Dazzling Women Designers

The Women's Hall of Fame Series

Dazzling Women Designers

Jill Bryant

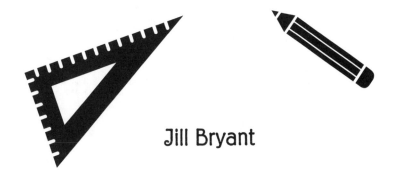

Second Story Press

Library and Archives Canada Cataloguing in Publication

Bryant, Jill
Dazzling women designers / by Jill Bryant.

(The women's hall of fame series)
For ages 9-12.

ISBN 978-1-897187-82-1

1. Women designers—Biography—Juvenile literature.
I. Title. II. Series: Women's hall of fame series

NK1174.B79 2010   j745.40922   C2010-904360-X

Editor: Sheba Meland
Designer: Melissa Kaita
Cover photos and icons © istockphoto.com

Printed and bound in Canada

*Second Story Press gratefully acknowledges the support of the Ontario Arts
Council and the Canada Council for the Arts for our publishing program.
We acknowledge the financial support of the Government of Canada through the
Book Publishing Industry Development Program.*

ONTARIO ARTS COUNCIL
CONSEIL DES ARTS DE L'ONTARIO

Canada Council   Conseil des Arts
for the Arts   du Canada

Mixed Sources
Product group from well-managed
forests, and other controlled sources
www.fsc.org Cert no. SW-COC-002358
FSC   © 1996 Forest Stewardship Council

Published by
Second Story Press
20 Maud Street, Suite 401
Toronto, ON
M5V 2M5
www.secondstorypress.ca

For Mari, whose imagination is an inspiration.

# CONTENTS

Introduction

Design is all around us. You can find it in our homes, our schools, our parks, and on our streets. Everything you see that was made by people was designed. Each new design begins as an idea—a flash of light that flicks on in a designer's brain. It evolves into a rough sketch, sometimes drawn on a napkin, or a scrap of wood, or a computer screen. Then, through many revisions, failed prototypes, and intricate models, the idea slowly transforms into something three-dimensional with form and substance. Something real that people will use.

Think for a minute about the look of a human-built object, something a person has crafted. Does it much matter what that notebook or flashlight looks like? Now, give that object a second glance. Consider its shape, form, style, color, sound, and texture. Does it sparkle, or rumble, or feel good in your hand? Does that please you? Lastly, judge the object by its usefulness. Does it work? Does its design enhance its function? Good designs do. The look and feel of a desk, cushion, vacuum cleaner, or mp3 player is important, even though you may not notice it immediately. It is as important as the way it works. It is part of the way it works.

At some point, you may have yearned for something (e.g., a certain pencil case or T-shirt) because everyone at school has one. Or perhaps you value individuality, and prefer to seek out one-of-a-kind items that no one else has. Whatever the case, you can't deny that the way a thing looks is important. But no matter how good it looks, if you buy something attractive, like a cool water bottle for instance, and the seal leaks the first time you use it, then that design is a failure. It is a double failure, because now the water bottle—bought to encourage eco-friendly living—is going to end up in the landfill after one use. Designing products carries a deep social responsibility. Designs must be functional to be effective. Part of the beauty of any design is the excellent way it works.

Design is a profession where the boundaries of art overlap with those of science, engineering, and technology. There are many kinds of design—from furniture and textiles, to fashion and architecture. Designers need tremendous problem-solving abilities. Strong math skills complement their drawing abilities and allow their imaginative ideas to be realized in concrete and glass, paving stones and peonies, metal and wood, or cotton and silk.

The ten women you will meet in this book are world-famous designers, renowned for their outstanding achievements. These designers have earned their fame through their imagination, daring, hard work, determination, and admirable strength of character. They are all people who think outside the box.

There is an amazing variety of designers and design fields across the globe. This book profiles women from Japan, India, Iraq, Senegal, Canada, the U.S., and the UK. Indian fashion designer Ritu Kumar and Senegalese textile designer Aissa Dione both possess a tremendous pride in their cultural roots, which is clear in their designs. English furniture designer Eileen Gray, who lived in Paris, and Iraqi-born international architect Zaha Hadid, were both unafraid to experiment with new materials.

This international list also spans a century of time. No matter when they worked, where their cultural roots lie, or what their field of design is, all ten designers share a common need to try bold ideas, and to express themselves with beautiful forms, lines, and shapes. Good design is universal and timeless.

In addition to facing gender challenges within their fields, some of the designers in this book experienced extra hardships that shaped their careers. Landscape architect Cornelia Hahn Oberlander had to flee her homeland with her family when their lives were in danger. Urban planner Jane Jacobs was arrested during a demonstration to stop the construction of an expressway. Designer Ritu Kumar's first collection of garments, which took her many years of planning and effort, was a failure. For most of her career, car designer Suzanne Vanderbilt earned less than her male co-workers. Graphic artist and costume designer Eiko Ishioka endured insults from male rivals. Fashion powerhouse Vera Wang gave up an Olympic dream shortly after she and her partner lost an important figure skating competition. Textile and furnishings designer Aissa Dione struggled financially to keep her unique company afloat. Dedication, passion, and perseverance kept these women striving to attain their goals.

> Have a look at several Canadian designers who've made their mark around the world:
>
> - fashion designer **Marilyn Brooks** (1932 –)
>
> - women's clothing designer **Linda Lundström** (1952 –)
>
> - furniture and housewares designer **Martha Sturdy** (1942 –)
>
> - rug-designing duo **Carol Sebert** (1957 –) and **Donna Hastings** (1957 –)

Without a doubt, it is difficult to choose just ten designers from a long list of incredibly talented candidates. There are many other brilliant women designers who have made a big impact on the world. Take a trip to the library or search the Internet to find out more about other women designers. In "Sources & Resources," at the end of the book, you'll find websites, books, and videos that feature more information about the designers you are about to encounter. By exploring the actual designs these women have created, you'll gain insight into their amazing talents. Even better, perhaps you'll find yourself inspired to try out your own special design ideas. But for now, read on, and prepare to meet some truly dazzling women of design.

—Jill Bryant

Eileen Gray

Simple Forms and Sharp Contrasts
1878 - 1976

Tall, striking, fashionable, and from a well-to-do family, the young Eileen Gray could have settled into a comfortable and easy life in southeastern Ireland where she was born. Instead, she took risks, moved abroad, and followed her heart. Unlike most women of noble status, she discarded her title, "the honorable Eileen Gray," and some of the social privileges that went along with it, and opted for a life devoted to work, art, and design. In time, she became both a celebrated furniture designer and a talented architect.

Eileen was the youngest of five, and because her siblings were all much older than she was, she didn't have any playmates among them. Nor were there any near the enormous, ivy-covered manor house where she lived. At night, the huge, old house—named Brownswood—seemed spooky to her. During the daytime, she often went for long walks by herself, on paths among rolling hills and along the banks of the River Slaney, at the edge of the family's property. Eileen enjoyed exploring the tumble-down walls of ruined castles nearby, and marveling at the beauties of nature.

Eileen's mother, Baroness Eveleen Pounden Gray, came from an upper-class family, with lords and ladies adorning her family tree. Eileen and her siblings took their mother's family name because of its high status in society. Baroness Gray was rather stern and serious and acted as the head of the family. Eileen's father, James MacLaren Smith-Gray, was a landscape and portrait painter who eventually took his wife's name, as well. He was charming, well-dressed, and free-spirited; of her two parents, Eileen was closest to him. However, her parents spent more and more time apart, as Eileen grew older, and before long they were living in separate countries. (At this time, it wasn't common for married couples to divorce.)

Eileen was allowed to visit her father wherever he was— Italy, or Germany, or somewhere else in Europe. She adored these trips abroad. They were a great escape from the boredom of tedious lessons and life at home in rural Ireland. This privileged Irish child was no stranger to travel. Her family divided their time between their country home in Ireland and their city townhouse in London, England.

Throughout Eileen's childhood, Baroness Gray hired governesses, who taught Eileen good manners, polite conversation for all social occasions, and how to stand, sit, walk, and dance with good posture and grace. Wealthy families in Victorian times didn't see the need for girls to study academic subjects. Instead, a lot of importance was placed on manners, fashion, and good taste—essential qualities for becoming a wife and the hostess of a grand household. Eileen's various governesses also tutored her in the basics of reading, writing, and arithmetic, and taught her about art and music.

Eileen attended a boarding school in Germany for a little while, to study art and music, but her formal education was often interrupted. Formal education just wasn't a high priority for girls. As an adult, this lack was something she regretted.

When she was feeling relaxed, young Eileen was known for her delightful laughter. As she grew older, this lovely laughter stayed with her, and while she was always a bit shy, she developed a mischievous wit as well. With her smartly tailored clothes and very refined manners, Eileen often appeared to be older than she was. In her late teens, she wore her long, dark auburn hair pinned up, and topped with a fashionable hat. She developed a passion for shoes and had a large collection to complete her striking outfits. Young men flocked around Eileen, but she wasn't interested in marriage. At the age of twenty-two, not too long after her dear father had died, she and her mother traveled to Paris. She was impressed by how exciting this city was compared to conservative London.

Eileen now had her sights set on a career in art, and convinced her mother to let her attend the Slade School of Fine Arts, in London. While it wasn't acceptable for women to study math or science, studying art was considered perfectly respectable for rich, young ladies. Her mother agreed, and Eileen moved to her family's London townhouse. Eileen's serious training as an artist was about to begin, and she was more than ready. As well as attending crowded classes at art college, she and her classmates often visited local galleries and museums. Their teachers encouraged them to copy the styles of famous artists, to help them learn how to paint using different techniques.

London had—and still has—some of the most important art galleries and museums in the world. Eileen was very impressed by the Victoria and Albert Museum. Focusing on art and design, this museum has huge and colorful collections that span several centuries, and many different art movements and periods, right up to modern times. There are fascinating displays of ceramics, glass, textiles, furniture, housewares, jewelry, and fashion, along with art gallery exhibits of paintings, photography, and sculpture.

It was here, wandering through the Victoria and Albert, that Eileen first saw marvelous folding screens, or room dividers, that were finished to perfection with a shiny lacquer. She admired their gleaming beauty, and immediately understood that they could add great impact to a room. The fact that screens were works of art that also had a function made them especially attractive to Eileen. With her head full of ideas, she was determined to learn how to make those screens.

In 1902, at the age of twenty-four, Eileen took a second trip to Paris. At this time and into the '20s and '30s, Paris was the home of many great artists, both French and from other countries. Irish novelist James Joyce and playwright Oscar Wilde were living there in 1902; American poet Gertrude Stein joined this group soon after. Eileen, like many other artistic people, was star-struck with the lively, bohemian energy of Paris and decided she had to move there. Cars were just becoming popular—Eileen bought one, then found an apartment with two friends. The trio attended an art school for foreign students and Eileen chose to focus on drawing classes, but found many of the exercises boring. A couple of years later, Eileen moved to another apartment with enough space to work in. She was lucky, because her mother helped her pay the expensive rent. With a place of her own in a city filled with young artists, Eileen felt as if nothing could hold her back from pursuing her dream of creating artistic household objects.

Eileen set out to find a lacquer work teacher and soon settled on a talented Japanese craftsman named Seizo Sugawara. She eagerly apprenticed with this young man, learning how to mix the perfect lacquer from a certain type of tree resin. The process required great patience and was extremely time-consuming as the lacquer took a long time to harden. Up to forty coats had to be applied, and between each coat the lacquer was sanded smooth with a type of porous volcanic rock called pumice. Color was added between the last layers, after sanding.

Always the perfectionist, Eileen often strove to achieve a certain shade of luminous blue and sometimes made the same piece over and over, even though she developed lacquer disease, a painful rash that is hard to heal. Her lacquer screens weren't plain, but they certainly didn't follow the formal décor styles of the time. Victorian-influenced rooms tended to be packed with dark, ornately carved furniture, rich fabrics (such as velvet and silk), floral patterns, and animal prints. For her decorative motifs, Eileen borrowed from ancient zodiac signs, incorporating these stylized symbols into her lacquer work. She sometimes imitated African art in her abstract designs. Like many artists of the time, Eileen also took much inspiration from the East in her early work.

When Eileen met a distinguished, influential, and rather high-strung art collector named Jacques Doucet, big things started to happen for her. Doucet owned many original paintings by masters such as Picasso, Rousseau, and Van Gogh, and a vast collection of one-of-a-kind furnishings that were also works of art in their own right. After spotting

> ## Lacquer
> The art of lacquer work, which gives wood a glossy coating that resembles thick, clear plastic, began in ancient China, India, and Egypt. Its beauty is timeless. For more than a hundred years, decorators have chosen shiny works of lacquer—in the form of elegant and ornate boxes, tables, desks, mirrors, picture frames, serving trays, and musical instruments—to introduce elements of Asian art to home décor.

In Private Life

Though Eileen Gray mainly moved in quite wealthy circles, she felt compassion for the poor and always gave money to charities. She loved animals, too. She couldn't bear to see an animal suffering or left out in the cold. Although she devoted her life to creating beautiful objects, she wasn't materialistic. She hated possessions, and preferred having only the essentials.

one of her exquisite lacquer screens, Doucet asked Eileen to make lacquer picture frames for his collection of Van Goghs. She found this work boring, but Doucet was very pleased, and in time, he commissioned Eileen to make some special pieces of her own design for his studio. He urged her to use the finest materials available, which made Eileen very happy. But then disaster struck. Some of the door panels she had designed especially for Doucet's apartment were featured in a magazine before Doucet took possession of them. When he saw the magazine, Doucet threw a massive tantrum and cancelled his order. The formidable Jacques Doucet, with his discriminating eye for superb design, wanted nothing to do with any object that ordinary people had already seen. He feared that others would rush to copy the work, knowing that it had his stamp of approval. Then, the copies would become readily available and the original in his collection would decrease in value. Doucet insisted that everything in his collection remain mysterious, hidden—and thus highly prized by other collectors—until such time as he, Doucet, decided to sell it.

Without all the attention from Doucet, the quiet Eileen might not have become such a talented lacquer artist. Doucet had a knack for discovering new artists and designers, and helping to launch careers. He was, however, quite demanding and he often meddled with the artists' work and creative process. When Eileen designed the Lotus table for him (the lotus is a kind of white or pink water flower, often featured in ancient Egyptian, Buddhist, and Hindu art as a sacred symbol), Doucet requested that she add large, heavy, decorative, green silk tassels. Eileen disagreed with his suggestion, but he was the client and was paying for the table, so she obliged—reluctantly. A whole fifty years later, gazing with regret at the Lotus table on display in a design exhibition, Eileen remarked, "If I had a pair of scissors, I would cut off those horrible tassels!" Though she was reserved and quiet, she was not one to forget her strong opinions about the look and design of her pieces. As a creator, she was never completely satisfied with her designs. She continued to criticize her pieces and try to perfect them, even when they were already on display in museums as celebrated works.

Years later, in 1972, long after Jacques Doucet had died, the furniture Eileen had made for his apartment received a lot of attention in the art world and the media. Finally put up for auction, Doucet's one-of-a-kind furnishings, made by some of the most renowned designers of the 20th century, fetched enormous amounts of money.

Art Deco

From about 1925 until the 1940s, a new style called Art Deco was all the rage in design. This style, which originated in Paris, was based on geometric shapes, zigzags, lightning bolts, and elegant curves. While Eileen never fully embraced this style, her rugs featured geometric shapes and were among the first examples of this emerging art movement. Some Art Deco designs included classical figures and motifs, such as the lotus flower. The main materials used were aluminum, lacquer, stainless steel, mirror, glass, and contrasting shades of inlaid wood. Three-dimensional designs, for everything from skyscrapers to radios, were streamlined and shiny. Bold patterns, high-contrast colors, and shimmering glamour characterize this period in art history. Many cities still contain elements of Art Deco design in their architecture.

As Eileen gained more confidence in her abilities as a designer, she decided to open a shop of her own. It was too challenging to earn a living from custom-design work. Her mother, who had been her main support, had died in 1919, and Eileen needed to attract more clients. The doors to Galerie Jean Désert opened in 1922. Eileen just made up a man's name for the shop, thinking it sounded more serious than her own name. Perhaps she believed the public wouldn't take a woman designer seriously. After all, she was the only female designer in France! Because she was a shy and modest woman who wasn't very good at promoting herself or her work, it's possible that staying out of the spotlight made her more comfortable.

Like exclusive art galleries today, Eileen's shop held only a few pieces at a time. She was not interested in producing pieces quickly. She worked slowly, with an eye to perfection for each creation. Eileen hired a woman to take care of the shop so that she could focus on her art. But business was slow. Eileen was an artist, not an entrepreneur. She didn't know how to run a store well and she didn't have much talent for making cheerful small talk to potential customers. Despite her lack of business sense, people did seek out Jean Désert, where they could buy her stunning furniture, geometric rugs, screens, and lacquer work. She pioneered built-in shelves, hidden cupboards, multi-purpose furniture, and reversible and extendable designs. Her customers included famous writers, artists, and politicians. The shop stayed in business for nearly ten years, but Eileen closed its doors in 1930.

Although she didn't have formal training as an architect, Eileen, who was already middle-aged, began designing houses in the south of France. She had a clear vision of the look she wanted and even without training was able to create excellent designs that builders could easily construct. She preferred to make little cardboard models of her architectural plans, rather than drawing accurate blueprints. She often sought advice from established architect Jean Badovici. He was the first to write extensive magazine articles about Eileen's work. This helped create a buzz in the art world about her unique designs. Eileen's friendship with this influential figure made her push herself artistically and technically, expanding her design work from furniture into homes with her signature streamlined look. When Badovici asked the excellent question, "Why don't you build?" Eileen was willing to accept the challenge.

This marked the start of an exciting, new path. Badovici asked Eileen to collaborate with him on designing and building a modern house for him in the fashionable Saint-Tropez area, in the south of France. Eileen chose a site on a wild, rocky peninsula overlooking the Mediterranean, and Badovici approved. He said he would help, but in the end, he didn't contribute too much. As editor of a highly respected architectural magazine, he was busy keeping tabs on the design world, writing articles, and meeting with prominent architects. Badovici was quite happy to leave Eileen to her own devices regarding the Saint-Tropez home.

To help her with technical issues, Eileen apprenticed under a Russian-Polish architect. She was too embarrassed to ask any of the prominent architects in France for advice. Instead she studied quietly and began to learn by doing; that is, by building her first house. Eileen named this house E.1027, which was alphabet and number code for her initials (E.G.) sandwiched around a similar code for Jean Badovici. (Hint: Count the letters in the alphabet—A = 1, B = 2, etc.) This house was perhaps Eileen's greatest architectural achievement, though she didn't ever view it that way. She considered this house, completed in 1929, an experiment or prototype, not a final, finished product.

Although Eileen Gray was a hugely influential designer whose work defined a whole new style in furniture and

A replica of Eileen Gray's E.1027 side table

architecture, she didn't receive much recognition or fame until the last two years of her very long life. Outside of her small group of friends, patrons, and mentors, Eileen was not part of the elite, inner circle of designers and architects. Being the only woman working in a male-dominated world had definite challenges. Her upper-class background also set her apart from other artists, who tended to struggle financially. It didn't help that she never signed her work, was shy, and often kept to herself. If Eileen had been more outgoing and interested in important connections and media opportunities, perhaps she would have achieved more recognition in her lifetime. Of course, if she had spent more time socializing at parties and public events, perhaps she would not have created quite so many unique works of art.

Today Eileen Gray is celebrated as one of the most important designers of the 20th century. Her E.1027 Side Table, overstuffed Bibendum Chair, and other superb, timeless furniture designs are mass-produced and sold around the world to those who love fine furnishings. Her original Dragon's Armchair sold for $28 million dollars when fashion designer Yves Saint Laurent died, and his collection of one-of-a-kind pieces was auctioned. Eileen Gray's name is synonymous with the terms "modern" and "avant garde." She turned old principles of design upside down, and forever changed the way we look at furniture and living spaces.

Jane Jacobs

Friend to Neighborhoods
1916 - 2006

For Jane Jacobs, one of the most original thinkers on the life of cities ever, an absence of traditional knowledge was a blessing in disguise. Her fresh perspective allowed her to see clearly what others could not. Instead of getting bogged down in lofty theories and intricate blueprints, Jane used her finely tuned powers of observation—and a healthy dose of common sense—to guide her vision for a vibrant, well-balanced city. Rather than accepting the idea that city dwellers must change their ways to fit a shiny, structured, and orderly modern plan, Jane celebrated the messiness of real city life, shining a spotlight on the real value of treasured little neighborhoods, great meeting places, and multi-use areas. Busy urban spaces, used for all kinds of things, formed the basis of Jane's vision for a workable, successful city.

Born Jane Butzner in the coal-mining city of Scranton, Pennsylvania in 1916, she always thought fondly about her first- and second-grade teachers, who taught her the basics of reading, writing, and math—and, more importantly, who ignited her thirst for learning. Unfortunately, her love of learning began to fade as she continued through school, and Jane started to play pranks to pass the time. By the time she reached high school, Jane was often bored. She used to sneak books under her desk to read during class. She said, "I just did enough to get by, really." Jane graduated from high school in 1933. Surprisingly, for a woman who went on to become a public intellectual, she didn't earn any post-secondary degrees or diplomas. (Over the years, she turned down about thirty honorary degrees that universities tried to present to her for her outstanding contributions to the field of urban planning.) After high school, Jane volunteered as a journalist for the local newspaper, *The Scranton Tribune*. She assisted with the "women's page" of the paper, bringing her fresh ideas and keen insights to readers in the community.

A year and a half later, during the Great Depression, Jane moved to New York City. Jobs were scarce and times were tough. Jane lived with her older sister, and they were so poor that they sometimes lived on a diet of baby food and bananas. (Powdered baby food was invented in the 1930s and was enriched with nutrients.) They made themselves swallow this bland food week after week because they knew it was nutritious and would keep them healthier than some other meal choices.

Jane used her free mornings to apply for extra jobs, and spent her afternoons walking around the streets of New York, watching people and feeling the pulse of this bustling city. These walks were the starting point for her informal education in urban planning. In fact, people watching became a crucial part of Jane's work as her career developed. She understood that it is people who make cities work, and that figuring out what people need, and keeping people happy in comfortable, workable spaces, was the most important idea in effective urban design. Without observing people, it was impossible to know which aspects of the city needed improving, and which should remain as they were.

Jane worked sporadically as a secretary for five years, and slowly began to get some journalism work. She wrote freelance articles for *Vogue, Harper's Bazaar*, and *Fortune*, and *The New York Herald Tribune*. Her writing focused on the different kinds of work being done in various parts of the city. For *Vogue*, Jane wrote about areas in the downtown core that related to fashion and décor, such as the diamond district, the flower district, the leather district, and the fur district.

When she was out of work, Jane took an assortment of courses in geology, zoology, law, political science, and economics at Columbia University in New York. Her marks were excellent and she thoroughly enjoyed her classes. After two years, however, the university started pressuring her to take specific courses to fulfill degree requirements. Jane wanted to take courses that interested her, just for their own sake. In the end, Columbia reviewed her file, saw her poor high-school marks, and asked her to leave. Jane was actually relieved. She thought this would let her spend more time getting a "real" education—that is, learning more about what she wanted to learn. It seems quite likely that

Though she was not a natural classroom student, Jane was an avid reader her whole life. She often read two or more books at a time, and liked to fill her home library with books on a wide range of subjects.

When she was 73, Jane published a children's book called *The Girl on the Hat*, which she wrote for her grandchild, Caitlin.

Jane—with her independent, unconventional ways of thinking—just didn't fit in well with the rules and expectations of formal institutions. Her best learning still occurred on the streets and in the parks and public spaces of cities, where she could observe how people interact with the environment around them.

When she was twenty-eight, Jane married architect Robert Hyde Jacobs, Jr., whom she had met while working at the Office of War Information. The year was 1944. They married in the living room at Jane's family home in Scranton. For their honeymoon, the couple set off on an exciting bicycle trip though Pennsylvania and New York. Jane Butzner became Jane Jacobs, and for the next twenty-four years the couple made their home in Greenwich Village, a lively inner-city New York community that attracted students, artists, and musicians. There they raised three children: Jimmy was born in 1948; two years later, their second son, Ned, was born; and their daughter, Mary, was born soon after that.

This was an era when cars were bigger and shinier than ever, when everyone dreamed of a house with a lawn and a white picket fence. The Depression was over, the war was over, and city planners were keen to get rid of the old and bring in more of the shiny new—whether it be the latest streetlight design or a new shopping mall. Modern designers had captivated the nation, and old things were looked on with scorn. Unfortunately, "old things" included grand 150-year-old stone mansions, historic Victorian rowhouses, heritage libraries, majestic banks, and cozy limestone cottages.

Through her exposure to her husband's work, Jane became increasingly interested in the field of architecture. She coupled this interest with her writing skills and was hired as associate editor of the magazine *Architectural Forum* in 1952. With her keen eye for detail and her writing skills, she became a valued member of the journal. Jane wrote about new architectural plans by renowned architects, but she often found that she didn't like what she saw. These modern designs often paid no attention to the way an area in the city actually functioned—the very essence that made it livable and lively. Jane thought most of these new urban plans

One of the first questions Jane always asked was whether the city was being built for people or for cars. She was opposed to zoning restrictions that squelched multi-use neighborhoods, and that sometimes tried to keep children quiet and off the streets.

were unrealistic. She especially disliked the way they ignored pedestrians and favored cars. Jane realized that politicians, who commissioned the city plans, spent little time considering the long-term growth and development of cities. Jane opposed this shortsighted view, which often resulted in bulldozing very comfortable, traditional neighborhoods to make room for highways, skyscrapers, and huge open spaces. There was almost no discussion of the consequences. Because Jane's articles were almost always critical of New York's new building projects, they prompted a great deal of controversy.

Jane's own children made a stand when the sidewalks on their street were threatened. Little Ned asked a surveyor what he was doing, and the surveyor explained that the chalk marks on the pavement showed where they were going to widen the road and remove the sidewalks. Ned told his brother Jimmy, and Jimmy couldn't get to sleep. When Jane asked Jimmy what was wrong, he told her he was upset because they would also lose a favorite climbing tree in front of their house. Jane listened carefully, hearing the children's concern. She was concerned too! None of the neighborhood residents had been informed about this plan. The very next morning, Jane helped Ned and Jimmy write a petition, and they took it to a print shop down the street. When the shop owner heard what the petition was for, he dropped his other work, and printed up the petition within an hour. Word spread quickly across Greenwich Village, causing an uproar. This grassroots effort, led by Jane and her children, saved the sidewalks of their neighborhood and defeated City Hall.

In the 1960s, Jane, who was now middle-aged, worked even harder to oppose "urban renewal"—a process that basically involved ripping up old, established residential neighborhoods to make way for new roadways, office towers, and parking lots. The pace of urban renewal was speeding up. When politicians argued that their new models of city planning would result in economic gains for the nation, Jane was quick to point out and promote the reverse point of view. She believed that strong city economies, based on vibrant communities, should come first, and that, in time, they would lead to a financially stable country.

With much encouragement and support from her husband, Jane put all her ideas on paper. She published her first book, *The Death and Life of Great American Cities,* in 1961. She was forty-five years old. Though she went on to write many more, this is still one of her best-known books. The groundbreaking study of urban planning begins with this opening sentence: "This book is an attack on current city planning and rebuilding." Throughout her life, Jane Jacobs's opinionated writing motivated her opponents to stop, think, and reconsider.

Jane Jacobs argued in that first book that the city should be seen as a living

In Halifax, Nova Scotia, between 1964 and 1970, homes in the 130-year-old community known as Africville were bulldozed one by one, in the name of urban renewal. Seventy families were left homeless, and—even worse—their history had been erased. It is true that the community was getting run down, but restoration might have been a far more humane solution, in line with Jane Jacobs's philosophies. This practice of mass demolition has occurred in other cities as well.

being, not an abstract thing. She described the streets in a neighborhood as the venue for a "sidewalk ballet," where many activities mingle harmoniously. Jane outlined four crucial components for a vital neighborhood to function well. First and foremost, she believed that every community should have several different functions that worked simultaneously. She preferred short city blocks that encourage pedestrians to take a variety of routes home each day, and allow them to patronize local shops and businesses. Buildings in a neighborhood should vary in age, style, and use. Jane liked highly concentrated population areas, with the diversity of households that

Jane Jacobs with her son Ned, her daughter, and her husband in 1968

Jane's tireless opposition succeeded in putting a stop to the plan for a Lower Manhattan Expressway in New York City and the Spadina Expressway in downtown Toronto. Her hard work and that of those she inspired allowed established neighborhoods to thrive and prosper.

this often brings. Rather than having a district where all the buildings are detached homes for middle-class families, she celebrated a more random mixture of families, students, elderly people, artists, entrepreneurs, and new immigrants.

One advantage to Jane Jacobs' mixed-use streetscape is that crime diminishes. If couples and families live above stores on city streets, people are on the lookout for unusual activities. In this way, residents are always watching the street, and crimes are more likely to be reported. Similarly, criminals will be less tempted to commit crimes, fearing that someone nearby may be looking out a window or sitting on a porch. Another advantage is that each group can gain new perspectives

Jane Jacobs and Toronto social activist June Callwood in 2005

from the other, fostering better tolerance and understanding.

Jane was a passionate and skilled advocate for long-term city planning. She worked hard to save established communities and to stop municipal governments from building super highways through healthy neighborhoods. In 1968, she was arrested during a demonstration to stop the construction of an expressway through some lively parts of Manhattan. Later that year, she and her family moved to Toronto, Ontario. Their move was a response to the U.S.-imposed draft of young men to serve in the Vietnam War. Her sons were eighteen and twenty years old, which made them eligible for the army draft. Bob and Jane Jacobs disagreed with the war, and didn't want to take the risk of their sons being drafted. Bob found work at an architectural firm, and Jane looked forward to the move as an exciting adventure. Once settled in Toronto, she continued to speak out against shortsighted city planning and to advocate for the rights of neighborhood residents and businesses. Jane became a Canadian citizen in 1974.

> "I don't know who this celebrity called Jane Jacobs is—it's not me. You either do your work or you're a celebrity; I'd rather do my work."

> "The city has something to offer to everyone, since it is created by everyone."
>
> —Jane Jacobs

Creating a dazzling city requires more than futuristic towers and immense public spaces. Jane Jacobs understood this very well. She knew that designing a workable, lively city requires a deep understanding of the needs, habits, and wishes of the people who live there. She was determined and steadfast in her convictions about city design, and in time her thinking drew international admiration. She was a many-time recipient of grants from the Rockefeller Foundation's Urban

Design Studies research fund. The grant money helped her to finance the time she needed to write her first book and to do other research.

The elderly Jane was honored in 1997 by the City of Toronto with a conference called "Jane Jacobs: Ideas That Matter." At the end of the gathering, an award was created that honors citizens whose activities are enriching the city's vitality. Recipients receive $5,000 a year for three years.

After a long, productive life, Jane Jacobs died in 2006 just days before her ninetieth birthday, but the energy that she created still lives. About a year after her death, the Rockefeller Foundation created the Jane Jacobs Medal, to be awarded to individuals who make positive contributions to urban design in New York City—either for lifetime achievement or for "new ideas and activism." That same year the City of Toronto honored this great thinker again by designating May 4th, 2007 as "Jane Jacobs Day." Specially designed walking tours called "Jane's Walks" were held throughout Toronto, giving the public an opportunity to learn more about her vision, and to see the beautiful districts and buildings she helped preserve. In September of the same year, this event also took place in New York City. It seems that the spirit of "Jane's Walks" is infectious. Almost seventy cities now hold such walks, including: San Juan, Puerto Rico; La Paloma, Uruguay; Goa and Mumbai, India; Dublin, Ireland; and Madrid, Spain.

Jane Jacobs devoted her life to making sure that governments carefully consider their citizens' wishes in all urban renewal projects. Due to her many published books and articles, and her personal bravery, urban residents across North America are now consulted and involved in most city-planning decisions. This is Jane's most valuable legacy.

Cornelia
Hahn Oberlander

Green Garden Designer
1921 –

The arrival of spring stirs the heart of Cornelia Oberlander. The chill of ice and frost leaves the soil, buds expand and crack open, and colorful blossoms make the air heavy with scents. As a toddler and young girl in Germany, Cornelia loved gazing down at the sprinkle of water flowing from her watering can and seeping into the tilled soil so that her fragile seedlings would grow.

Cornelia's mother, Beate Hahn, was a horticulturalist, so she knew all kinds of things about plants, which she enthusiastically shared with her daughters Cornelia and Charlotte. Beate was passionate about fostering a love for nature in her daughters and in all children and even wrote gardening books for children—one of them featured illustrations of young Cornelia digging in the soil. Throughout her childhood, Cornelia needed no encouragement to spend time outdoors. She spent much of her time enjoying nature and had her own garden to take care of from the age of four. She usually grew corn and peas, her favorite vegetables.

When Cornelia turned eleven, following a tradition in her family, she visited the studio of a famous German artist to have her portrait painted. It was hard not to squirm as she posed for the artist, and her mind wandered. She wished she were swimming or climbing trees. As she sat with her head crooked to one side, resisting the urge to scratch her nose, she peered up at a large, colorful drawing on the wall of the studio. It showed the Rhine River and an imaginary town. Cornelia was intrigued by the different colors in the map-like picture. She asked the artist to explain it. The artist told her that the red shapes were houses and the beige marks, which extended to the river, represented streets. Cornelia asked what the green bits were, and the artist replied that they were parks.

While it's true that time can alter memories, Cornelia still insists that this moment in the artist's studio was what made her realize she wanted to design parks. During that moment, Cornelia experienced that same stirring in her heart that she'd

A landscape architect (LA) is a designer of outdoor spaces, including parks, playgrounds, lawns, gardens, and courtyards. LAs must analyze, plan, design, and manage the building of outdoor spaces. They must be good problem solvers. They have to consider drainage, elevation, light levels, soil conditions, and sustainability in their designs. LAs create detailed drawings, much like architectural drawings, to map out their designs. Their materials may include plants, shrubs, trees, flowers, paving stones, gravel, pebbles, rocks, benches, and sculpture. Five Canadian universities and more than sixty universities in the U.S. offer programs in landscape architecture.

felt as a young girl in her family garden. From this point on, Cornelia had a goal for her life. Her vision started to become real when, as a teenager, she met friends of her mother who were landscape architects. Cornelia may have been young, but her ambition was strong. She never faltered from pursuing her dream. She did become a landscape architect, and she has stuck with her beloved profession for more than sixty years.

Tragedy struck Cornelia's family just before she turned twelve. Cornelia's father was killed in a sudden avalanche, while skiing in the Alps. Though this was a heartbreaking and unsettling time for the family, Cornelia's mother remained strong, and as time went on, she even insisted that they continue taking ski holidays. She wouldn't allow the children to be consumed by grief.

Soon her father's death was not the only challenge facing the Hahns. Adolf Hilter was in power, and life was becoming increasingly difficult for Jews living in Germany under the Nazi Party's anti-Semitic rule. Cornelia's family celebrated both Christmas and Hanukah, but they were considered Jews in the eyes of the government. Mrs. Hahn sheltered her daughters from the ever-worsening racist policies of the Nazis, and kept them busy with all kinds of lessons, activities, and outings. Cornelia and Charlotte took English and French classes, competitive horseback riding, and trick riding. In spite of the troubled atmosphere around them, the girls still led calm and privileged lives.

When she was fifteen, the father of one of Cornelia's classmates disappeared. A shocked silence fell over the community. Everyone realized that the Nazis must have taken him away. A couple of years later, the situation had become steadily worse, and Mrs. Hahn knew that it was no longer safe to remain in Germany. Years earlier, just before he died, Cornelia's father had actually talked about leaving. Now, Mrs. Hahn made the plans, bought train tickets, and packed a few belongings from their large, comfortable family house. Sadly, Cornelia had to say good-bye to her dear grandmother, who wished to remain in her home country.

Cornelia was seventeen when she arrived in New York City with her mother and Charlotte. The year was 1939. Mrs. Hahn wasn't impressed with the materialistic values that character-ized the big city and wanted to protect her daughters from the attitude that money was everything. She decided to purchase a quiet farm in New Hampshire, and the three of them moved to this pretty rural spot. Here, Mrs. Hahn farmed vegetables successfully enough to plan on sending her two daughters to college. Cornelia could hardly contain her excitement about the prospect of studying landscape architecture. She talked all the time, to anyone who would listen, about how she was going to design beautiful parks and gardens. Mrs. Hahn was happy to channel some of her daughter's exuberance into something productive. Cornelia's new spare-time job was selling the farm's fresh produce in a nearby market town. Standing beside a truck full of vegetables, feeling her pockets grow heavier with coins, Cornelia stayed focused on her dream.

When it came time to apply to university, Cornelia's first choice was Smith College, in Massachusetts, but the elite insti-tution didn't seem to think she was suitable because of her thick German accent. The situation changed quickly, how-ever, when the administration saw that she had achieved an astonishing 96 percent average in high school. The admis-sions committee was impressed, and she was duly accepted at Smith. Cornelia studied botany, history, and art.

During a 2004 interview for the *Smith Alumnae Quarterly*, Cornelia reflected on college rules for women: "When I went to Smith, women who wanted to become landscape architects went to the Cambridge School, a part of Harvard University, because at that time, women could not attend Harvard. But with the war that changed, and in 1943 I was one of the very first women to be admitted to the Harvard Graduate School of Design." It was at Harvard, in 1945, at the Graduate School of Design school picnic, that she met her future husband Peter Oberlander. Peter was studying to be an architect and city planner. He was as keen and hardworking as Cornelia, and they both used to study day and night. In order to share time together, the couple often

Smith was founded as a women's college, and is still one of the best universities in the U.S. A number of its students went on to become famous. Chef Julia Child, activists Betty Friedan and Gloria Steinem, former First Ladies Barbara Bush and Nancy Reagan, and poet Sylvia Plath are among the women who studied there.

helped each other with school projects. Their similar interests in design and planning, and their ability to focus intently for hours and hours on their studies, bound them together.

Cornelia graduated from Harvard in 1947 with a Master of Landscape Architecture degree. The young landscape architect worked in Pennsylvania and New York. After she completed a playground design in Pennsylvania, *Life* magazine praised it for its fresh originality. The 1954 article says, "Designed to be pleasing in line, safe to use and stimulating to the imagination, the new playthings cater to the natural inclination of youngsters to climb like mountain animals, crawl through dark passageways and hang by their heels." Although the story didn't mention her by name, Cornelia was thrilled to receive such notice for her ideas, in a magazine that, in its time, had nearly the impact that CNN does today.

When Peter got work assignments in England and Canada, they were parted for a few years. Then, back in New York, Peter told Cornelia that he had accepted a job in Canada at the University of British Columbia, and they decided it was a good time to marry. They were wed at City Hall in 1953, then moved across the continent to Vancouver, where they have lived ever since. Cornelia—wasting no time in getting established—founded her own landscape architecture firm in the same year. Soon, she was back in the thick of things, designing park playgrounds, which had become her specialty.

Cornelia and Peter raised three children: Judith born in 1956, Timothy in 1958, and Wendy in 1960. Cornelia worked significantly reduced hours when her children were young. She enjoyed watching them build castles in the sandbox and play outdoors. While her children played, Cornelia continued to puzzle over the key elements of a perfect playground and park. She took note of what children naturally liked to touch, climb, manipulate, and build. She loved the way children were instinctively drawn to plants, trees, stones, and flowers. Cornelia was delighted to see the way her children interacted with the natural world—smooth pebbles, crystallized rock, gnarled sticks, snail shells, and pussy willow blossoms all captivated her young naturalists.

Cornelia was intent on caring for her children and took a central role in their upbringing. Juggling home responsibilities, childcare, and a career was a lot to manage, but Cornelia was

Early Women Landscape Architects

Although women make up only 34 percent of practicing landscape architects, there is a long history of pioneering women in this field.

Best known for her simple cottage gardens, **Gertrude Jekyll** (1843 – 1932) had a great influence on the use of borders, color, and rocks in garden design. She designed more than four hundred gardens, mainly in England. Today, some of her gardens have been restored, based on her original designs.

In exchange for leasing thirty acres of empty parkland in San Diego, California, **Kate Sessions** (1857 – 1940) agreed to plant one hundred trees in the park each year, and an additional three hundred in other parts of the city. She grew a wide variety of trees from seeds she imported from the tropics, including flowering jacaranda and eucalyptus.

very well organized, and had nannies to help when the children were babies and toddlers. The children attended day care centers before they started school, and the Oberlanders had a housekeeper come once a week to clean. Still, there were after-school activities to take the children to, groceries to buy, and meals to cook, as well as her work. Later in life, Cornelia jokingly rhymed off how many family meals she cooked: 143,000!

Cornelia said, "Observing my own children at play became the inspiration for the design at the Children's Creative Centre at the Canadian Pavilion for Expo '67." Cornelia was brimming with innovative ideas. She spent days creating detailed drawings for her unusual plans. This playground lacked the traditional swings and slides, and instead had many special areas that fostered interaction, and stimulated children to play. There was a tethered wooden rowboat that kids could climb into and pretend to row. There were stacks of logs that children could use to build structures. A massive chalkboard encouraged kids to draw, and a large pegboard featured strands of wool that kids could wrap around pegs to make string art. Nowadays there are strict rules and regulations guiding what features can be included in playgrounds, how high climbers can be, and what materials can be used. Even back in the more relaxed 1960s, many critics of the design feared that children might get hurt while playing. But Cornelia stood firm. Children needed to have places to dig, create, climb, balance, and build. These were enriching activities that would stimulate children's minds, and help develop motor skills and coordination. Thirty thousand children played in this Expo playground, and the only reported injury was one sprained ankle. Cornelia's playground design was a huge success.

By the age of fifty-three, Cornelia was well known for designing wonderful playgrounds and parks. Her children were growing up, and she could easily have coasted along for twelve years until retirement. But then the phone rang. It was Vancouver's City Architect Bing Thom, requesting that Cornelia attend a meeting about a huge project in downtown Vancouver. When Cornelia hung up the phone, she was buzzing with anticipation.

Cornelia met with Bing Thom and renowned architect Arthur Erickson. Arthur showed her plans for a fifty-storey building. After brainstorming and sharing ideas, Arthur considered laying the high-rise on its side. This would allow a large, horizontal roof garden to extend along the structure. The idea was extraordinary.

"Who in 1974 wanted a park on a roof? Nobody!" Cornelia recalled at a recent interview. Nonetheless, Bing and Arthur were receptive. Though she had never designed a roof garden before, Cornelia quickly and confidently listed her ideas for the plan on the spot. These included making the garden accessible to all people, and full of light and interest through all the seasons. Next, Cornelia described various technical requirements they'd have to consider for a functional and beautiful roof park. There was the importance of studying the weight on the roof, using an alternative growing medium (rather than soil, which is too heavy), addressing drainage, and waterproofing the roof to protect the inside of the building.

Needless to say, Cornelia got the job. She worked together with Arthur Erickson and drew up a stunning plan that fits well with the surrounding buildings and plantings to this day. The soil is made up of washed sand, volcanic rock called pumice, and composted food waste. Another environmental bonus is that the garden absorbs lots of rainwater, and this reduces the amount of water flowing into nearby storm sewers. In addition, the plants on the roof use up carbon dioxide and produce oxygen, which helps keeps Vancouver's air clean. Cornelia and Arthur designed this very forward-thinking project, called Robson Square, between 1974 and 1983. Cornelia is still very proud of the roof park. She admires the way the garden attracts office workers on lunch breaks to relax, enjoy nature, and chat with friends. Cornelia says, "Such spaces are essential for our cities."

Cornelia Oberlander and Arthur Erickson continued to work together on other projects. One journalist dubbed them "the A-Team of Canadian Landscape Architecture." The Museum of Anthropology at the University of British Columbia, designed by Arthur Erickson, was completed in 1976. Cornelia planned the outdoor spaces to partner perfectly with the building and its contents, which include an awe-inspiring collection of totem poles carved by the Northwest Coast peoples. The painters, weavers, sculptors, and other artists whose work is displayed in the museum, were Aboriginal peoples from the Queen Charlotte Islands. So Cornelia was inspired to choose grasses, ferns, and trees from the Queen Charlottes to set off the modern lines of the concrete and glass building, and to contrast with the dramatic surrounding meadows and forests.

Another major project was the National Gallery in Ottawa, designed by Moshe Safdie Architects in 1988. Cornelia battled hard for a northern Canadian garden to mirror the rugged subject matter of the Group of Seven's landscape paintings. The committee rejected her strong desire for jack pines, favoring the more popular Austrian pine species. Cornelia remained true to her vision, however, by selecting the most misshapen Austrian pines, to mimic the windswept jack pines found clinging to rocky outcrops on

Dynamic Duos

Throughout her successful sixty-year career, Cornelia Hahn Oberlander worked with world famous architects on elaborate projects. These giants of architecture include Estonian-American architect **Louis Kahn**, Canadian architect **Arthur Erickson**, Israeli/Canadian/American architect and urban designer **Moshe Safdie**, Italian architect **Renzo Piano**, and Latvian-American architect **Eva Matsuzaki**.

the Canadian Shield. When her plans were implemented at last, the reviews were highly favorable. Finally people understood her vision. Cornelia received the Canadian Society of Landscape Architect's National Award for her design work for the National Gallery.

The campus at the University of British Columbia contains Cornelia's beautifully crafted gardens at the Museum of Anthropology, and also the revolutionary green spaces surrounding the cutting-edge C.K. Choi building. This structure is special because it is the first environment-friendly building at the university. From the start, Cornelia issued a provocative challenge: "No trees will be removed during the construction of this building!" The team took up this radical idea and ran with it. The building is considered one of the top ten green buildings in North America. Cornelia sheepishly confides, "I'm pretty bossy. When I have an idea, then it's got to be done, you know?"

Completed in 1996, the three-storey C.K. Choi Building is equipped with space shuttle-inspired composting toilets. (Because water is heavy and costly to transport to space, space scientists have developed a way to reuse the water in astronauts' urine. This is the same remarkable technology that allows astronauts to drink their own purified urine.) The team of designers for the C.K. Choi Building wanted to be off the grid of the city sewage. They wanted to use plants to treat and purify the gray water that flushes down

---

Sustainable Design

Sustainable design has minimal impact on the environment, and ensures the well being of our grandchildren's grandchildren. For example, sustainable buildings reduce energy consumption (for heating, cooling, equipment, and lights) and use reclaimed and recycled building materials as often as possible. The C.K. Choi Building is made of more than 70 percent reclaimed materials, including salvaged wood and brick from demolished buildings.

---

all the toilets and drains in the building. After consulting with NASA officials, Cornelia designed a novel, environment-friendly filtration trench. Cornelia selected beautiful aquatic plants, such as irises, juncos, and sedges, which she planted in the trench that surrounds the building. To most onlookers, this trench of functional flowers resembles a simple flowerbed—and its design ensures that it isn't the slightest bit stinky.

Cornelia Hahn Oberlander has been called Canada's premier landscape architect, and a grand dame of landscape architecture. Many revere her like royalty, and for good reason.

Cornelia enjoying the fruits of her labor—the apple tree was planted when her children were young.

She has earned many highly prestigious for her ingenious designs, which attractively integrate sustainability with excellent materials and indigenous plants. She received the Order of Canada in 1990, the Canadian Society of Landscape Architectects' Lifetime Achievement Award in 2006, and was named an Officer of the Order of Canada in 2009. Cornelia has always been ahead of the times. She saw the importance of interactive playgrounds for children before they became popular. She recognized the value in shrinking a building's ecological footprint before climate change was in the headlines. She makes her designs accessible to young and old, and people with mobility challenges.

Cornelia is finally at the end of her illustrious career, but her work lives on. Aspiring landscape architects all over the world look at her achievements and find inspiration, in their simplicity, beauty, and thoughtful, tempered balance.

Suzanne E. Vanderbilt

Comfort and Styling
1938 – 1988

At a time when career choices for women were virtually lim-ited to nursing, teaching, and secretarial work, Suzanne E. Vanderbilt bucked the trend. "I really knew what I wanted to do, and that was to work with my hands as an artist," recounted Suzanne, looking back at her childhood.

She recalled that when she first told her mother about this ambition, and wanted to start art classes, the reaction was swift and negative. Suzanne's mother, a musician and piano teacher, was not at all supportive of her dream. "Deliver us from crazy artists!" she remembered her mother exclaiming in exasperation.

Instead of expensive art classes, her parents said they

would enroll her in less costly piano lessons, which her mother favored. Disheartened, Suzanne returned to the comforting atmosphere of the basement, where her father was repairing a wooden toy. From the age of six, Suzanne had always enjoyed working beside her father in his basement workshop. First she learned how to hammer nails into a block of wood. Then Suzanne's dad taught her how to use some of the beautifully made hand tools he collected, such as planes (for smoothing wood), chisels (for making grooves), and braces and bits (for drilling holes).

Born in Mount Vernon, New York, Suzanne grew up in a suburb of New York City called Larchmount. When she wasn't making things in the basement workshop, Suzanne was drawing—or playing baseball, football, or soccer with the boys in her neighborhood. There was only one other girl on her street, so Suzanne often played with the boys. She dutifully went to her piano lessons, but only because she had to. By the time she reached high school, Suzanne knew more than ever that she wanted to pursue art. She looked over the course offerings, and signed up for Mechanical Drawing. It sounded perfect for her, combining her love of art and her curiosity about the workings of things. Soon after, she was called to the office and told that girls did not study mechanical drawing, it was for boys only. When Suzanne quickly retorted, "Then why is a woman teaching it?" she did not receive an answer. The other art class that Suzanne could take that term focused on basic lettering. The aspiring designer enrolled, as this, she recalled, "was

> "As a child, I used to disassemble watches, clocks, toys, and anything that had a nut and bolt or screws to hold it together—I needed to know how things worked. With so many doors closed to women, I retreated to music—a proper ambition. It gave me a great background, and I use that now, but then I was heartbroken."
>
> —Suzanne E. Vanderbilt, in a 1985 interview

the only way I could get some feel for the mechanics of using a triangle and T square," the basic tools for mechanical drawing. Apart from coloring in lots of posters for student clubs and events, Suzanne didn't find any other opportunities to hone her design skills during high school.

This was especially disappointing because she'd had an important conversation with one of her father's friends when she was about fourteen. She told him that she was thinking about a career in illustrating for medical journals, but when he heard about Suzanne's interest in drawing, making models, and building things, he told her about the field of industrial design. She was very intrigued. As luck would have it, one of the Vanderbilts' neighbors had graduated from the Pratt Institute in Brooklyn, New York. She urged Suzanne to write to the head of the art school to find out more about their industrial design program.

Pratt was a top-notch design school that offered fundamentals such as sketching, concept development, researching various forms, and creating functional items. It was a great fit, and Suzanne started there after high school. To be accepted into Industrial Design, Suzanne had to complete one year in the basic design program with good marks. In addition she had to submit several drawings: one of an iron, another of a piece of furniture, a third showing her living room, and one more describing a personal experience. She applied, and was accepted into the program. Suzanne graduated from Pratt in 1955, after earning a Bachelor of Industrial Design degree. She was on her way.

After graduation, Suzanne was very excited to be hired for her first job by the General Motors design division in Detroit. In the 1950s, car design and manufacturing were male-dominated areas. The few women who were employed by car manufacturers were typically secretaries, clerks, or cafeteria workers. The management was entirely filled by men,

Industrial Design

This field of design involves planning and creating a wide range of three-dimensional products and parts of products for everything from cars, trains, toys and games, to household goods, electronics, musical instruments, and medical equipment. People pursuing this career path need excellent sketching skills and should have an aptitude for math and science. They should also understand the key principles of sustainability, which include using materials that are non-toxic, recycled, or reused; reducing energy consumption; incorporating durable construction; and impacting the environment minimally.

and the engineers, designers, and technicians were all male. General Motors' Vice-President Harley Earl had different ideas. He was responsible for design and styling and thought that women designers would bring a fresh, new look to GM's cars. Earl assembled a team of talented female designers to create beautiful car interiors, unique upholstery combinations, and special detailing options. Some of these women worked in the Frigidaire Production Studio—a GM subsidiary located in Dayton, Ohio—where they customized the details for refrigerators and washing machines. True to the times, much of what the women were hired to do was targeted specifically to women drivers and women's tastes. This stereotyping was common at the time.

All these intelligent, creative, and capable women were much more than "pretty faces"—they were bona fide industrial designers with college degrees, many with previous training in industrial design. Quite a few of the designers had graduated, like Suzanne, from the Pratt Institute. But it was unusual at that time for women to work in professions, other than in support roles, and when Harley Earl gave women this highly visible opportunity in industrial design, the media grabbed hold of the story. The all-women design team became a sensation, known from coast to coast. The "Damsels of Design," as GM and the press called them, suddenly found that they were celebrities.

When she started at GM, Suzanne was very eager to work on the instrument panel that houses the speedometer and other dials, but she wasn't permitted to do this until much later in her career. She and the other female designers struggled constantly with being viewed as lightweights. Their design work was most often restricted to fabric and color choices, when they were capable of doing much more. The media, with their write-ups about the glamorous Damsels of

Harley Earl poses with his automotive designers known as the Damsels of Design. Suzanne Vanderbilt is on the far left.

Suzanne Vanderbilt with interior design for the 1957 Cadillac Allegro

Design, didn't help either, and so the team constantly had to defend their industrial expertise. "We weren't there just to decorate," Suzanne recalled. "Unfortunately, the projects that were publicized were decorating." The opinion Suzanne held to, throughout her career, was that "good design should be for men and women."

Harley Earl retired from GM in 1958. This was a great loss to all women in the auto sector. Suzanne had a great deal of respect for him, and strongly believed that as the forward-thinking head of her department he had been "instrumental in getting women into design." The man hired to replace Earl— Bill Mitchell—was not nearly as progressive in his acceptance of women on the design team. Still, Suzanne and some of the other women held on to their positions.

Suzanne spent twenty-three years at GM, but her opportunity to rise to a managerial role came only because one of the bosses was injured in a car accident and was unable to work for a few months. While she didn't obsess about advancing in the corporation and "just wanted to be a good designer," as she said, Suzanne did realize that she was earning much less than men who held similar jobs. In order to earn a higher salary, she'd have to advance from Junior Designer to Senior Designer, and even possibly to Chief Designer. Suzanne set

---

Mary Anderson, inventor, 1866 – 1953

On a visit to Manhattan, Alabama native Mary Anderson noticed that streetcar drivers had to stop and wipe ice and snow from their windshields so that they could see the road. This problem got Mary thinking, and she sketched out her idea for a device with a spring-loaded arm, a rubber blade, and a lever. The manually operated device was effective, and Mary received a patent for her invention in 1903. Mary didn't earn much money for her invention, but her design was the basis for windshield wipers from the 1920s onward.

her sights on this seemingly impossible goal, and got ready for the challenge. She did have a competitive streak, and her persistence was steady. In 1961, her perseverance paid off when she was named Assistant Chief Designer of the Cadillac studio at GM. Soon after, she decided to improve her credentials by pursuing a Master of Fine Arts degree at Cranbrook Academy of Art, near Detroit, Michigan. The auto manufacturer wasn't too happy about this at first. In the end, however, GM gave her a full tuition scholarship, with Suzanne's word that she wouldn't leave the company for good.

At Cranbrook, Suzanne enrolled in design, then switched over to metalsmithing to learn about casting and forging metal. She found the program enriching, and returned to GM in 1965 with lots of energy and enthusiasm. What she found, however, was that she would have to start all over. She was being demoted from Assistant Chief Designer to Senior Designer. At this time, Suzanne's job was limited to doors, seats, steering wheels, knobs, and some details on the instrument panel—not the technical instruments she longed to tackle. It took four years for Suzanne to rise to her previous level at GM. She had to work extremely hard, taking on additional responsibilities in the hope that some day she'd be promoted.

With so much experience behind her, Suzanne resented still being called on for interior styling jobs, such as choosing fabrics and colors. She later commented that it "should not have been beneath any of the men" to choose colors and fabrics, but she did as she was asked. She continued earning less money than her male counterparts, and didn't feel this was fair. But as there were not yet any laws to ensure pay equity, there was nothing to be done. Finally, after undergoing an on-the-job test, which she passed, she was promoted to Chief Designer of Chevrolet *Interior II*, where she designed small cars. It was a first for GM, and for women designers everywhere. She had stuck it out, and made it.

Suzanne's ongoing passion for design was evident in her love of stylish sports cars and fine home décor. Her car of choice was a sporty and curvy Corvette. She had a keen eye for design and aesthetics, but also was concerned about safety and comfort. In 1967, Suzanne designed an inflatable seat back support that helped lessen back pain while sitting. She held the patent for this device, which was ahead of its time. Over her career, she also designed a collapsible safety switch for the instrument panels on cars, and a motorcycle helmet.

In 1971, Suzanne Vanderbilt was promoted to the position of Chief Designer of General Motors. This was an enormous achievement. At long last, she could also afford to buy a condominium. With this new position, however, she had to get to work very early for meetings, and work longer hours than ever, often until late into the night. Her enormous responsibilities covered the whole company's design initiatives. This meant her job was even more deadline-driven and stressful than ever. But she took it all in stride.

Health challenges came her way in 1973. Suzanne underwent surgery for cancer and had to take some time off work for chemotherapy treatments. Because she required more rest and needed further treatments, Suzanne stepped down to a far more junior position. She became a design assistant so that she could work a four-hour day. Then,

Industrial Designers to Watch

Joann Jung, part of Ford's design team since 2004: "I design for the person's lifestyle."

Denise Gray, director and engineer, Energy Storage Systems at GM (part of hybrid battery development team since 2006): "I have always felt the need to bring something different to the table."

Crystal Windham, industrial design manager at GM and 2007 Car-of-the-Year winner at the North American International Auto Show: "I always want to produce something that's not already out there."

> "It was a designers' paradise, and we particularly enjoyed proving to our male counterparts that we were not in the business to add lace doilies to seat backs or rhinestones to the carpets, but to make the automobile just as usable and attractive to both men and women as we possibly could."
>
> —Suzanne E. Vanderbilt

needing still more time off due to her poor health, she decided to take early retirement in June, 1977. She was not yet forty years old. Toward the end of her time at GM, it bothered Suzanne that she wasn't known simply as a designer, but as a *"woman designer."* Speaking of the female designers at GM she said, "we designed the same as the men did."

Suzanne's illness interrupted and cut short her unique accomplishments in industrial design. Sadly, she died at the age of fifty, when many designers are just reaching the pinnacle of their careers.

Suzanne Vanderbilt felt the higher purpose of a designer was to "enhance the world with whatever contribution you can make…" It was her passion and her calling.

"Design," she said, "is my whole life."

Eiko Ishioka

Fantastical Designs for Stage, Screen, and Beyond
1939 –

A young Japanese girl kneels on a mat in the living room of her family home. According to her own ritual, she carefully unfolds the waxy brown paper of a candy bar wrapper to reveal the words "Hershey's Milk Chocolate." She holds the paper up to the window and examines the play of light through the special wrapper, noticing how it changes the appearance of the English letters. Smoothing the paper on her knee, she traces the outline of each letter with her finger, knowing the shapes by memory. Her lips curl into a small smile as she delights in the crinkly texture of the paper packaging. Nothing has ever seemed more beautiful to her than this American candy bar wrapper.

"Aren't you Japanese?" chides a stranger in a restaurant one day, seeing her admiring the English words on the chocolate wrapper.

"Why are you reading that and not a picture book?" asks a neighbor who has come to visit.

Eiko looks the person in the eye and says, "Why not? What's wrong with that?"

The visionary, multi-talented Eiko Ishioka was born in Tokyo, the capital of Japan. As a young child, she was used to spending a lot of time alone. She used to get teased by other kids, because she had different interests from most. She didn't really care about fitting in, however, and had her own ideas about what games she wanted to play. Amazingly, she didn't let the taunts of her classmates dampen her spirits. She was an independent, strong-willed girl who was fueled by an active imagination. Eiko was lucky to be raised in a supportive home environment, where she was encouraged to go her own way by her artistic and open-minded parents.

Many Japanese families follow the tradition of having a stay-at-home mom. This is part of the culture. When she was young, Eiko's mother had wanted to be a professional, but her mother had told her that she'd never find a husband if she followed an academic path, so she had given up her ambitions and become a housewife. Now, when it came to her own daughter, Mrs. Ishioka went against the traditions and encouraged Eiko to pursue a profession. Eiko's father, who was a gifted and acclaimed graphic designer in the early days of this new field, agreed. By the time Eiko was seven, she was already intrigued by her father's job. It seemed likely that she would follow in his footsteps and pursue a similar career. She also found in her youth that while she was not talented in sports, the display of human strength and athletics greatly fascinated her.

All through elementary and high school, Eiko kept her

focus on art. After graduating, she became a student at the Tokyo National University of Fine Arts and Music. Always ambitious, she knew that learning English would give her more freedom to work internationally, so she added that to her classes. She studied hard, and wanted to do well. Strangely, her father now tried to convince her to pursue a different path, perhaps because he knew the challenges and hardships she might face. The life of an artist or designer can be uncertain. This didn't deter Eiko, however, and right after she finished her degree, she wasted no time in setting up shop as a graphic designer. Throughout her career, Eiko always said she was inspired by her father's creative spirit. Years later, when her father died, Eiko believed that his creativity lived on in her, and she continues to credit him with her growth as an artist.

When Eiko was in her twenties, in the 1960s, her first clients were Shiseido, a major Japanese cosmetics company, and Parco, an exclusive department store. Right from the start, she was successful in designing for advertising. In fact, before the end of the decade, she won several awards in Japan for her striking graphics. Her unique designs made a strong impact, and she was gaining recognition very rapidly.

With her fame, came jealousy, however. In a 1990 British article published in *The Times*, Eiko explained that "male rivals used to say I was only famous because I was a woman, a novelty. I promised myself then that I would become so obviously special in my field that they would have to shut their mouths." These strong words show a fiery side of Eiko—a side that kept her going. She faced more challenges because she was a woman and in the minority—especially in the traditional society of her homeland. In all likelihood people thought that once she got married, she would quit her job. But it turned out that she didn't marry, and she certainly didn't stop working. She went on to create a myriad of superb and varied works over the course of a five-decade career.

Postmodernism

This 20th- and 21st-century movement challenges conventional views in art, literature, and design. Postmodern art may include aspects of classical or traditional style, but they are "deconstructed", or taken apart, to reveal their parts and their contradictions. Artists explore meanings, but there is no such thing as universal truth. Mixing components from many different cultures and beliefs is the norm. So is irony. An example of a postmodern children's book is *The True Story of the Three Little Pigs* by Jon Scieszka.

In 1979, Eiko rocked the design world with her groundbreaking postmodern poster for the film *Apocalypse Now*, directed by Francis Ford Coppola. The poster depicted helicopters flying over a massive wave (and a tiny surfer), with bold Japanese script across the bottom. The art by Suriyama borrowed its wave image from the classic Japanese woodblock print, "The Great Wave off Kanagawa" by Hokusai—a 19th-century masterpiece known throughout Japan and in many other countries.

In 1983, Eiko published a book called *Eiko by Eiko*. This large-format coffee-table book is filled with glossy photos of her advertising images, many of which center on the human body. The book opens with stories about Eiko by friends, colleagues, collaborators, artists, and designers. All these different anecdotes bring Eiko's complicated personality and bold philosophy to life. When movie director Paul Schrader found and read this book, he was immediately captivated by Eiko's point of view. He invited her to be the production designer for one of his upcoming films, *Mishima: A Life in Four Chapters*, about the life of the brilliant and troubled Japanese writer Yukio Mishima. Eiko asked, "Why me?" Paul responded by saying that he wanted a new visual concept and was very taken with Eiko's fresh approach to design. "I had no formal technical training in costume design, production, or film,"

Eiko remarked. Despite this, she decided to go ahead.

During the filming, Eiko confessed that she loved the excitement of working in the movies. The film opened in 1985, and Eiko won an award for it, in the category of Artistic Contribution, at the Cannes Film Festival. Her very first experiment in the film industry had been highly successful. Much more was to come.

In spite of her friendship with a fashion designer, Eiko regarded costume design as dull, passive work— basically taking creative direction from others. About her personal approach, she remarked later: "passive is definitely not my style." So, when the esteemed director Francis Ford Coppola asked Eiko to design costumes for his movie, *Bram Stoker's Dracula*, her response was negative and blunt: "I am not [a] costume designer." Francis altered Eiko's impression of costume design when he looked her in the eye and said: "I want the costumes to be the set of this film." Elaborate, Victorian period costumes, made from exquisite, rich fabrics, would have a central importance to the script, he told her. In the hands of Coppola, this was to be a lavish, sophisticated horror movie—he would be the first to make such a film. (As a rule at that time, horror films were low-budget and unlikely to win awards; they were typically over-acted, unconvincing, and of poor quality.) Not only would the costumes convey the essence of each character, but they would also convey the mood of each scene.

> Eiko finds inspiration in her hero, Michelangelo—the immortal Italian sculptor, painter, and architect of the Renaissance. Michelangelo is most famous for his sculpture *David*—which celebrates the beauty of the human form—and for his magnificent paintings on the ceiling of the Sistine Chapel. He created works according to his clients' specifications, but maintained a signature style that admirers could recognize in an instant. Eiko respected his individuality very much.

Eiko was intrigued, accepted the job, and immediately began immersing herself in the script, reading about Dracula, vampires, and Victorian fashions. But as with her other projects, Eiko didn't stay focused on the obvious. Instead she drew inspiration from many different cultures as she worked on the look of the costumes. Coppola provided input, suggesting, for example, that Eiko look at Klimt's famous painting "The Kiss" for one of Dracula's robes. Klimt had applied gold leaf and oil paint in a patchwork of colored circles and rectangles to produce a richly textured effect. It was this rich texture that Coppola wanted Eiko to mimic, and she thought this was a wonderful idea. Their collaboration had begun.

Eiko spent five months working with costume design assistants to brainstorm and sketch ideas for the film. Eiko insisted on high-quality costumes, so good that they could later be displayed at a museum. As a result, very costly fabrics were used for the garments, which were made by skilled costume makers using exquisite hand-sewing and embroidery techniques. (As costume designer, Eiko conceived the ideas and made sketches, but she didn't do the actual sewing.) The costumes were hugely expensive to create. In many cases, in order to save money only one gown or suit was sewn, even

Catwalk Theater

Eiko is a long-time friend and client of Japanese fashion designer Issey Miyake. She admires Issey's designs, which—like her own work—blend East and West. She loves his pieces so much that she often wears them over and over until the elbows are threadbare. Eiko says that on the rack, his clothes look lifeless—it is the wearer that transforms Issey's garments into beautiful works of art. On one occasion, the friends combined their skills to create a brand new kind of fashion show. This Issey Miyake fashion event, more like an avant-garde musical extravaganza than a traditional catwalk show, dazzled audiences lucky enough to see it.

though having duplicates was the norm and would have made life easier. The cast had to wear the same outfits for days. Instead of having duplicate costumes to switch to, the crew had to constantly wash, iron, and mend the finely constructed outfits to keep on schedule.

Eiko devised Dracula's red Oriental-Turkish robe with a gold coat of arms. To come up with an image, she drew on her early-career experience designing logos for corporations and ad campaigns. Rather than solely mimicking coats of arms from Scotland and European countries, she looked to her Japanese heritage in creating a fictitious family emblem that also looked like the crests featured on Japanese family shields. Eiko is especially adept at blending ingredients from many cultures to create something unique that captures the desired mood. In Francis Ford Coppola's essay titled "An Artist Who Knows No Boundaries," which appears in the book *Eiko On Stage*, he writes that Eiko's work "transcends cultural boundaries on many levels." Coppola goes on to say that he appreciates her "refreshingly different viewpoint." Looking at things differently is a big advantage in the field of design.

After the film's release in 1992, *The New York Times* reported, "Costumes do not get any more exquisite than this." When Oscar time came around, Eiko won the coveted Academy Award for costume design. In the same year, Eiko was inducted into the Art Directors Club Hall of Fame in New York. She was making bold statements and being met with enormous praise in the design world. Working in film was very exciting, indeed.

The year 2000 marked the release of the third film in which Eiko took part: *The Cell*. This psychological thriller, directed by Tarsem Singh, features a doctor (played by actor Jennifer Lopez) who "travels" inside the body of Carl, a killer, to join his nightmare-like world. In this monstrous place, the costumes are otherworldly, offering great scope for Eiko's imagination. From a luxurious flowing gown, to skin-tight suits

> Eiko directs and designs music videos as well. She finds "the marriage of music and visuals really exciting."

with strange ribbing, the costumes are rich, intriguing, and bizarre. Eiko was enormously pleased and challenged by this project.

True to her ongoing appreciation for athletics and super-human feats, Eiko was thrilled to design sleek and aerodynamic racing uniforms and outerwear for the Swiss, Canadian, and Spanish teams for the 2002 Winter Olympic Games in Salt Lake City. The suits featured state-of-the-art technology researched by Dr. Ruth Morey Sorrentino. Silicone bumps and spirals enhanced stability and reduced drag. Eiko also directed costume design for the closing ceremony at the 2008 Olympics in Beijing.

Eiko has a good friend in Francis Ford Coppola. When Eiko was in her early sixties, he invited her to watch a performance by Cirque du Soleil, thinking Eiko's skills would be a great match for the fantastical settings of Cirque shows. She loved it, of course. In the meantime, Cirque director Dominic Champagne came upon Eiko's book *Eiko on Stage* in a bookstore. He was attracted to the skin-tight, red-veined costume worn by Jennifer Lopez that was featured on the book's cover. Dominic was starting to develop the show *Verekai* and was looking for new talent. Eiko was on his list! The connection between Eiko and the other creators was instantaneous, and this marked the beginning of an exciting, new journey for Eiko.

As always with her costume designs, Eiko looks for meanings and themes to match each character. This approach is in stark contrast to conventional fashion design, which tends to rely heavily on trends. Eiko built her jewel-toned, fantasy-creature costumes based on such animals as lizards, birds, octopus, and other underwater creatures. The main challenge in designing for Cirque, however, was creating costumes that were visually stunning, and also safe for the performers. If a costume embellishment or detail caused a performer to falter or trip, the costume would instantly be rejected. Eiko took this aspect very seriously. Tests assured safety in the costume designs and fabric choices long before the performers tried them out. Rather than letting this challenge restrict her designs, she found ways to work with it. She created breathtaking costumes for *Varekai*, which opened in 2002 and has toured forty-six cities around the world. Eiko's costumes enhanced the performers' physical feats by making their acts look even more impressive than they were. And, yes, there

An Eiko Ishioka costume from the 2006 movie, *The Fall*

were costumes that featured bizarre projections that stuck out from the skintight leotards like giant, pointy scales, but these extra parts moved with the performer and didn't get in the way of movement.

> Eiko says, "I never stop expanding my challenges."

In Eiko's chic, downtown apartment that features massive windows overlooking New York—one of the world centers for design excellence—the look is minimalist. She once told Francis Ford Coppola that she needs "a clean space to think." Accordingly, her home and creative sanctuary is sparsely decorated, uncluttered, and serene. Eiko is often inspired by nature and likes to observe the play of light on people and things. But the ever-present hum of "New York City, the stunning array of people," also infuses her work.

Eiko Ishioka is celebrated as one of the best designers of the 20th century. It's extraordinary that one person can conjure up such a wealth of concepts in so many different forms of artistic expression, from graphic design and costume design to advertising, opera, film, and live performance. Eiko is an amazingly original thinker. Who knows what will come next from her lively genius?

Ritu Kumar

New Look; Old Design—Reviving India's Textile Heritage
1944 –

Italian, French, English, and American designers domi-nate the international stage for fashion design. Until fairly recently, few designers from developing countries made it to the international fashion circuit. Rather than embracing new styles adapted from their own rich cultural heritage, fashion-able women in countries such as India were often enticed by Western designs. But a fascination with Indian design, beginning in the 1970s, has changed all this. Ritu Kumar, the "grand woman of Indian fashion," rekindled a desire for nearly forgotten, traditional hand-sewn arts, and was a key player in the movement called fashion revival.

Ritu was born in 1944 in the city of Amritsar, in the region of India called the Punjab. Her birthplace is famous for its Golden Temple and is the holiest city for Sikhs. (Men of the Sikh faith can often be recognized by the turbans they wear to cover their heads.) When India reclaimed its independence from the British Empire in 1947, part of the country became what is now Pakistan. Amritsar is located right on the border between these two nations, and as a result, the city experienced some unrest and conflict in the late 1940s, when Ritu was a young girl, just starting school.

Ritu was fortunate to attend Lady Irwin College, in New Delhi, and graduated with an arts degree in 1964, when she was just nineteen. That's quite a bit younger than most people graduate from college or university. This women's college is in the lively center of New Delhi, near art galleries, special museums, and beautiful performing arts centers. It was an inspiring atmosphere for Ritu during her teen years. Graduates of this college have frequently attained top executive positions in leading Indian businesses and international organizations. Like Ritu, many have pursued careers centered on fashion and the arts.

Ritu married in her early twenties but this didn't curb her academic pursuits. An eager, enthusiastic student, Ritu next earned a Bachelor of Education degree. She moved from

Revivalism

In this movement, lost textile arts, such as block printing and traditional hand embroidery, are brought back into demand, and become popular. There is a strong preference for handmade products over machine-made goods. This rekindles employment for craftspeople, which can help the economy of regions and improve the lives of impoverished artisans and their families. This movement sees people reconnect with important parts of their local heritage, and the excitement can spread around the world.

New Delhi to Kolkata (formerly called Calcutta) and joined an amateur theater group. In 1966, Ritu left her home country and set off to another women's college, for graduate studies in art and history. The college, called Briarcliff, was in the quiet village of Briarcliff Manor, in New York state. She was twenty-five years old upon graduation. Not yet ready to end her formal education, Ritu returned to India to enroll in a museum studies program. She studied at Ashutosh Museum and became passionate about the history of clothing in India. She was especially fascinated by the many different methods of embroidery that were used to decorate fabric.

After completing this program, Ritu felt that she wanted to start her own business and put all her knowledge to work. In a small village near Kolkata, she started to create traditional designs for women's clothing, using cotton, silk, leather, and a set of rustic hand-block printers. Soon Ritu opened a shop and began establishing herself as a fashion designer and strong advocate for the lost crafts of India.

As she worked, Ritu craved more knowledge about India's nearly forgotten textile arts. Many techniques were dying, because India's royalty and high officials no longer needed such exquisite custom-made costumes. During Britain's ninety years of rule in India, the Maharajas and other members of royalty had been allowed to keep their titles and their enormous wealth. But instead of holding power and ruling their states, the duties of the royal class were confined to partaking

> **Museology**
>
> Not to be confused with musicology, the study of music, museology is the study of museums. Curators of museums—who organize the exhibits and research items in the museum's collection—usually have a graduate degree in museology. Artifacts from the past fascinate people who work in museum studies. Ritu, who studied museology, had a particular fascination with historic textiles and costumes.

in traditional rituals and ceremonies. After independence in 1947, the British left, and the finances of India's royalty crumbled. Former Maharajas turned to careers in business, hotel management, and politics. They had no need of elaborate traditional dress. Twenty years later, when Ritu had completed graduate school, there was almost no demand for the skills of master craftspeople. In addition, the artisans, discouraged by a lack of work, weren't teaching new apprentices their skills, to ensure they would be passed on to the next generation.

Ritu traveled to different regions in India where various techniques were still practiced to some degree. She was impressed with the pride of elderly craftspeople, who had learned these arts from their grandfathers or grandmothers. Ritu was happy to see these techniques, which were very time consuming and required a great deal of patience, still existed. She decided that she wanted to use these ancient methods in her own clothing designs. If she was successful, this might create employment for these skilled laborers. There was a small group of educated, worldly Indians like her, who had a dream of rekindling traditional crafts. Ritu realized that if they could spark enough interest, the demand for handcrafted fabrics and garments would increase. Fortunately, the Indian media were sympathetic. Influential reporters helped spread the message, and more and more people began to see the value and beauty of supporting and celebrating India's historic crafts.

Ritu launched her first fashion show of thirty saris, all modeled on historic textiles. She only sold twelve of them, though the show went on for several days. Very disappointed, Ritu thought hard about why her designs had failed. Finally, she realized that the stiff, heavy fabrics—some could have been used as wall hangings or bedspreads—did not work for modern fashion. Ritu had to figure out how to maintain the spirit of traditional fabrics, but design in a way that fit in with modern looks. This humbling experience taught Ritu a great lesson: Never try to design without a vision based on real life. It was back to the drawing board—literally. Ritu began to sketch plans for designs that incorporated traditional motifs and historic patterns, but with appeal for stylish, urban women.

Ritu continued her historical research for many years. During this time there were other significant and happy events in her family life. Rita had two sons, Ashvin and Amrish. Even when her children were young, Ritu and her husband continued to travel extensively, as was their habit. Their children joined them on most of these trips around India and abroad. As Ritu's career blossomed, the number of trips abroad increased. Her boys became accustomed to exploring new places and to having a well-known mother.

While Ritu's imagination continued to find fresh forms for old patterns, something interesting was happening in the fashion districts in Kolkata and Mumbai. Her new-old fashion designs took off in a really big way. Professional women loved Ritu's clothing line for the styles, colors, and patterns, and for the way the designs demonstrated such a sense of national pride in their cultural heritage. Not overly decorative or ornate, and featuring just touches of gold and glitter, Ritu's new designs had sophisticated subtlety, stunning silhouettes, and gorgeous colors that won her high points with her adoring fans. Ritu explains her carefully honed vision in this way: "My woman is international and global, yet rooted in Indianness. My line has a mix of Indian motifs on modern silhouette patterns. It reflects that women now have their own ideology and individuality when it comes to dressing up, and are not fashion victims."

Ritu is most known for her traditional designs, but she makes both traditional Indian clothing (such as saris, kurtas, and salwar-kameez) and Western styles (such as dresses, skirts, and blouses). She describes this ability of Indian designers like herself as "multi-dexterous" and thinks this is why so

Some Traditional Indian Textile Arts

If you've ever seen Indian elephants weighed down with thick, elaborate, shiny, tapestry blankets on their backs, you've seen *zardozi* embroidery. This age-old, Persian art form (Persia includes modern-day Iran), is hand stitched by craftspeople—usually Muslim men. Rich fabrics, such as velvet and silk, are appliquéd with gold and silver threads, then adorned with pearls and precious stones. *Zardozi* techniques were used for the clothes of royalty, ornate wall hangings, bedspreads, and cushion covers, in addition to decorative cloths for animals on parade.

The ancient technique called *bandhani* results in vibrant color patterns through tying and dyeing cloth. An artisan marks the pattern on fine bleached muslin with wooden blocks, and vegetable-based dyes extracted from onions, marigolds, red cabbages, and indigo. Next, the tiny shapes in the block prints, such as circles and flowers, are pulled and tied. The craftspeople dye that part of the cloth in a bright color. Then the fabric is tied and dyed again in one or more further bright colors. Finally, the border of the cloth is dyed. The more times the cloth is dyed, the more complex the designs. The end result looks much like a simple embroidery pattern. Today, chemical dyes are commonly used.

Craftspeople who do *chikan* work begin with hand blocks to stamp designs on the fabric. Then they hand-embroider the designs. The traditional style features white embroidery patterns on white fabric. Today, other colors of thread are popular, too. The embroiderer can use a variety of stitches, from chain stitch to hemstitch, to create different effects. The roots of mirror work, called *shisha*, trace back to Persia in the 1400s. Hand-sewers incorporate tiny mirrors into spectacular embroidery designs. Sometimes tiny, round mirrors are used for eyes in peacocks or for the centers of vibrant flowers. Other shapes, such as triangles, squares, and diamonds, are common, too. Craftspeople stitch around each mirror shape to hold it in place on the fabric. *Shisha* is featured in eye-catching clothing and accessories, and for textiles, such as bedcovers and cushions in home décor.

many Western designers and manufacturers, such as Italy's Gucci and America's Tracy Reese, are flocking to India for inspiration. Ritu's skills as a designer shine most in her bridal collections. Three- and four-piece wedding ensembles vary according to the Indian region they represent. The decorative borders and necklines of traditional Indian bridal wear showcase the finest handwork of the country's artisans. The colors of her bridal wear vary from solids in shades of cream, soft rose, and deep red, to exotic, multi-colored palettes of shimmering tangerine, purple, raspberry, and fuchsia.

In 1999, Ritu published twenty years of fruitful research in her lavish book, *The Costumes and Textiles of Royal India*, which celebrated the story of historic Indian clothing designs. She began with the research she had conducted in her twenties, and built on that. She sought excellent examples of different garments, and highlighted regional differences in the designs and techniques. Centuries ago, each region of India was renowned for its own styles and techniques. Kashmir, in the far north among the Himalayan Mountains, was famous for its weaving; the finest silk came from Varanasi; gold embroidered garments came from Lahore in Pakistan; and soft, delicate muslins came from Dacca. All of these sumptuous fabrics were fashioned into garments worn by kings, queens, and other members of the royal family. While researching, Ritu looked for surviving historic garments that could be photographed and shown in her book.

When it launched a Fashion Week in the late 1990s, India finally achieved world-class fashion status. India Fashion Week has steadily grown in popularity and success. It now attracts designers from around the globe who want to see what Indian designers have on offer, and which fabric suppliers and specialized hand-sewing techniques can be commissioned. Prior to India Fashion Week, foreigners mainly viewed India as a fabric supplier. But now, top international designers have

Ritu Kumar on the runway at the 2009 Eco Week in New Delhi, India

incorporated traditional Indian motifs, such as paisleys, into their collections, and have borrowed historical styles of Indian ornamentation as well as its jewel-tone and metallic color combinations.

> **Fashion Advice**
>
> According to Ritu, these are the must-have items for a stylish Indian woman:
>
> - 1 beautiful sari
> - 1 pair of black pants
> - 2 blouses
> - lots of scarves in different colors
> - some unique pieces of jewelry

About this new and exciting shift in taste Ritu says, "I think now what is happening is that people are looking towards India to source—not because it's cheap, but because it's special, and I think that's a very, very important difference." The local textile industry was brought back to life thanks to the efforts of visionaries in India like Ritu who established organizations such as the Handloom and Handicraft Boards and the National Institutes of Fashion Technology. Now sixteen million craftspeople across India enjoy increased income by proudly recreating textiles and embellishments from the time of their ancestors. This combination of art, culture, and economics is unique to India.

Ritu launched her new line, "Label," in 2002. In this collection, with its wispy and flowing shapes, she strives for a "cut, color, drape, and feel of the garment" that is pleasing to the modern woman. Her youngest son, Amrish Kumar, worked with his mother on this new label.

Ritu's other son, Ashvin, is a filmmaker and director. Ritu—who clearly enjoys working with her sons—has done the costume design for some of Ashvin's films. She also designed costumes for the Canadian film extravaganza *Bollywood/Hollywood* (2002). Unique arrangements for these films freed Ritu from being on set for days on end. She did the research, designed the costumes, and then got back to her fashion lines—that's where her heart is. Over time, scores of her popular boutiques had opened across India and one was launched in the United States.

In 2008, French Ambassador to India Jerome Bonnafonte presented Ritu with France's Knight of the Order of Arts and Letters Award for her contributions to Indian fashion. The ambassador showered her with these accolades: "Ritu Kumar is keeping alive the cultures of India. The history of the fashion industry and the history of culture is the history of human civilization."

Ritu takes pride in being an excellent role model and mentor for aspiring designers in India. It's no surprise that she was named president of the Fashion Design Council of India. Amazingly, she's been working as a fashion designer for fifty years—and counting. Always keeping up with the latest in fashion, she can reliably be found—impeccably dressed, and with a bright, warm smile—in the audience of Indian fashion shows, big and small.

Ritu has never forgotten the passion she experienced in witnessing elderly artisans working on looms in rural villages. For helping to revitalize these forgotten crafts, and for her creativity and perseverance, she truly deserves to be called a fashion icon.

Vera Wang

From Blades to Bridal Wear—Building a Fashion Empire
1949 –

The old expression "born with a silver spoon in your mouth" means that wonderful opportunities come your way due to your family's wealth and influence, not through your own hard work. In the case of Vera Wang, whose father was a wealthy tycoon, she could easily have slipped into living this cliché. But even though her parents were rich, they still believed in the importance of working hard to achieve your dreams, and they instilled this belief in their children.

Vera Wang was born and bred in New York City. Her parents were born in Shanghai, China. Her father, Cheng Ching Wang, was the son of a prominent military general. Her mother, Florence Wu, was the privileged daughter of a

> "For me the idea that I could always do better, learn more, learn faster, is something that came from skating. But I carried that with me for the rest of *my* life."
>
> —Vera Wang

Chinese warlord. As a young woman, Vera's mother completed a university degree before her marriage in 1939. After World War II, the couple moved to the United States, where Florence worked as a translator for the United Nations. Cheng Ching started his own businesses and built up enormous wealth.

Growing up on the exclusive Upper East Side of New York with her younger brother Kenneth, Vera's childhood was one of privilege and opportunities. Her parents bought her lovely clothes, sent her to the esteemed Chapin School in Manhattan, and enrolled her in ballet and figure skating lessons.

Vera adored the gracefulness and flowing lines of both skating and ballet. Skating at Madison Park Gardens with a private coach kindled her first real passion. She started skating when she was eight years old, and she was crazy about it. Before long, Vera began competing. She won lots of medals, and it looked as if the Olympics were in her future. Vera trained hard throughout high school, skating ten hours a day during the summer holidays, and up to six hours a day during the school year. Her coach could see that she was competitive by nature. She trained hard to win.

Vera excelled in pairs skating. She and her partner, James Stuart, took fifth place in a junior pairs competition at the 1968 national ice-skating championships. Vera and James showed promise, but they weren't number one. Soon after, James decided to pursue singles skating, which left Vera without a partner. Pairs figure skaters have to train for months and years with their partners in order to compete at high levels. Vera was devastated. Her Olympic dreams were dashed, in spite of her very hard work. She briefly considered a career touring as a show skater, which is a popular choice for many figure skaters who have retired from the competitive circuit, but Vera felt that this wouldn't be fulfilling. She was too ambitious. Vera hung up her skates and pondered what to do next.

Vera started off majoring in drama at Sarah Lawrence College, just north of Manhattan—one of the top arts colleges in the U.S. She thought acting would be similar to the theatrical side of figure skating. She became disillusioned, however, when she wasn't cast in any lead roles. Vera realized that this was the unfortunate reality in the 1970s for a female Asian actor like herself.

She faced this new setback with a positive and practical attitude. Besides skating, she realized she had another passion—her second love was for fabulous clothes. Her parents appreciated the value of high-quality garments, and her mother, in particular, had always followed fashion enthusiastically. And so, Vera decided to change her college major to art history—a good foundation for budding designers. She was setting her sights on a career in design, and the very idea was exciting.

Part way through her studies, she had the opportunity to spend a year studying at the Sorbonne in Paris. International students have always been attracted to this historic and renowned university, which offers exchange programs with many colleges around the world. It focuses on studies in the Humanities, such as music, art, and the classics. While studying at the Sorbonne, Vera lived in her parents' luxurious apartment, not far from the home of legendary fashion designer Yves Saint Laurent. Her mother, who loved Paris, joined her daughter for this interesting year abroad. Mrs. Wang took her daughter shopping at Chanel, Yves Saint Laurent, and other designer boutiques. Vera also accompanied her mother to the seasonal fashion shows of prominent designers. This is where Vera began to soak up the basics of French fashion design.

Back in New York, Vera took on summer jobs working at the Yves Saint Laurent boutique as a sales clerk and a window dresser. When she finally told her parents that she was seriously interested in pursuing design, her father objected. He wanted her to go into law or business. Vera was upset. Fashion design was the center of her universe now. Her father wasn't offering to pay for design school, and Vera couldn't pay for it herself. She needed to come up with a plan.

Without further delay, Vera polished her resume, and made some phone calls. A contact at *Vogue* magazine helped her out, and to her delight she was hired as an assistant editor. As soon as she landed this job, Vera worked tirelessly to learn about the fashion industry at "Boot Camp *Vogue*." She was a devoted assistant, a fast learner, and very capable. She never had to be asked twice to do anything. She didn't even mind running out for yogurt or coffee when the models needed a break. Vera was enthusiastic and fit in well in the fast-paced workplace. She coped calmly with exacting demands and a great deal of stress due to frequent deadlines. Even as an entry-level employee at *Vogue*, she frequently worked from 9 a.m. until 2 o'clock in the morning. Her hard work and talent

Designers Who've Rocked the Fashion World

In 1965 when the Beatles were crooning "Yesterday" over the airwaves, Mary Quant popularized the mini skirt. She also designed mini dresses and short shorts called hot pants.

Vivienne Westwood's punk rock designs sent shock waves through the 1970s fashion scene. Corsets, safety pins, tartan, and leather characterized this look that is still a favorite among rebellious fashion fans.

Katharine Hamnett brought activism to fashion in 1983 with her protest T-shirts. Messages like "Save the Whales" and "Stop Acid Rain" were printed in large black letters on her white Ts.

were rewarded. Vera was promoted to editor, and then to senior editor when she was twenty-three years old, making her the youngest senior editor on staff.

She attended fashion shows, met with designers, chose outfits for photo shoots, assisted with photo shoots, selected photos to run in the magazine, and developed themes and content for upcoming issues. Vera remained on staff at *Vogue* for sixteen years. When she realized she was never going to be promoted to editor-in-chief, Vera resigned from the magazine and in 1987 became the design director at Ralph Lauren. At last, she was well paid and beginning to try her hand at design. Vera designed accessories, lingerie, and sportswear, and enjoyed her new responsibilities and fresh creative challenges.

A few days before her fortieth birthday, in 1989, Vera married her long-time friend, computer executive Arthur Bekker. During her three-month search for a wedding dress, Vera became frustrated. The dresses she found in bridal shops were too showy, with too many flouncy ruffles and oversized bows. They seemed to be designed with younger brides in mind. She wanted a wedding gown that was sophisticated and elegant, a dress that would make a bold statement. Unable to find anything suitable in the boutiques of New York, Vera designed a $10,000 hand-beaded gown for herself, and planned a spectacular wedding for four hundred guests. Vera's wedding was covered by the *New York Times Magazine,* and the guest list included family, members of the fashion community, executives, and other high-profile figures. From the exquisitely crafted invitations and the hundreds of cream-colored roses to the elaborate place settings and the twenty-two-piece orchestra, Vera oversaw every detail. Getting married alerted her to the fact that there was a gap in the marketplace for sophisticated bridal wear. Ralph Lauren himself pushed Vera to fill this niche, and Vera was definitely thinking about it.

Vera and Arthur wanted to have children, but like many

While Ralph Lauren didn't sell bridal wear in the 1980s, he usually offered to design a gorgeous wedding gown for brides-to-be who were on staff. Ralph didn't make this offer to the very picky Vera. She humorously says that "if I didn't like it, I would have been in trouble." It was probably to avoid an awkward situation with his strong-minded staffer that Ralph Lauren tactfully refrained from getting involved.

couples in their forties, they had trouble conceiving. Vera quit her job at Ralph Lauren during this time. She had so many doctors' appointments, she felt she couldn't give her full attention to her job. Finally, Vera and Arthur adopted two girls: Cecilia (born in 1990) and Josephine (born in 1993).

In the meantime, Mr. Wang—always attuned to promising business opportunities—was intrigued by his daughter's plan to start a bridal line. Vera's father felt the timing was right, and he was willing to support her in this venture. Cheng Ching sat at his desk and happily wrote Vera a check for a staggering four million dollars. Delighted—and very grateful to her father—Vera bought a small boutique on Madison Avenue. Upscale boutiques require a polished look that projects their image and complements their style. Vera spent one million dollars of her father's investment to redecorate the building, and opened Vera Wang Bridal House Ltd. in September 1990.

From the start, Vera's shop offered brides advice on much more than choosing a wedding gown. The attendants in the boutique were trained to assist brides with other wedding details, from hair styling and flower bouquets to invitations. She liked making wedding planning easier for her discerning customers, and thought it was important to offer her clients the entire package. Later, as Vera's business prospered, she expanded her bridal line to include equally elegant invitations, footwear, jewelry, china, and crystal glassware.

In a Vera Wang wedding gown, brides can expect the most

sumptuous haute-couture fabrics. Vera loves to create texturing and layering using very fine fabric, such as tissue organza (made from finely woven silk for a sheer look), tulle (a starched net-like fabric used for wedding veils or tutus), and mousseline (a very fine cotton, rayon, or silk fabric that resembles gauze). With their luxury fabrics, pleats, and all-over gathering, Vera's gowns are often described

> "I am partially the person I design for. I think as a woman designer it's a very different experience than a man. Men are coming from a very abstract point of view. They're thinking of how they see a woman. And I think some of the women designers that I admire the very most are the women who *feel* what it is to be a woman in clothes. And I could cite them forever, starting with Coco Chanel."
>
> –Vera Wang

as frothy, airy, and light. Pushing the boundaries and endlessly experimenting, she became famous for developing "illusion netting," which simulates the look of bare skin, and asymmetrical gowns with different sleeve treatments, uneven hemlines, and angular special features. These unusual details result in a fresh look that is extraordinarily flattering. Brides flocked to her because Vera's dresses possess a simple elegance, unique features, and extra attention to detail that is unmatched by off-the-rack gowns.

It's possible, with a bit of luck, to find a simple Vera Wang wedding gown for just over $3,000, but many with detailed embroidery or beadwork fetch prices of $10,000 to $25,000 and up. With prices like these, it's no surprise that Vera Wang caters to the stars. She has designed custom wedding gowns for Mariah Carey, Avril Lavigne, Victoria Beckham ("Posh Spice"), Sarah Michelle Gellar ("Buffy"), and Chelsea Clinton. The most astonishingly priced was a gown for Jennifer Lopez, made for her marriage to Ben Affleck, which never took place. This unworn dress was a Vera masterpiece, and priced at

Designer Donna Karan chats with Vera Wang during
Mercedes Benz Fashion Week in New York.

$100,000. As Vera's business grew, she made the natural transition into eveningwear, and dressed such actors as Meg Ryan, Halle Berry, and Charlize Theron for the red carpet at the Academy Awards.

In 2001, Vera published *Vera Wang on Weddings*. This beautiful coffee-table book includes a photo of Vera on her own wedding day and showcases many of the wedding gowns that Vera has designed. Readers can learn the names of different types of skirts, sleeves, trains, and bodices of wedding gowns. One of the most amusing names for a style of bodice is "crumb catcher." This is a bodice that is starched to stick out from the body in a sort of rounded fan shape. (If the bride were to snack on a cookie, the crumbs would certainly fall inside the front of the dress.) This lavish book is meant to help couples create their dream wedding, and includes details about creating invitations, choosing flowers, and designing table arrangements.

> "I am a feminist. When I stop and think about it, there's no other way I can label myself. I am for women. I think some of the greatest designers have been men, but I think there are some for whom women are abstract. It's a design concept. Or it's some kind of fantasy or joke on women. Either way, it's not based on a real understanding of women and women's needs. I respect other women, and my clothes show it. I'm not making fun of them or trying to degrade them or make them feel silly. I'm trying, if anything, to make them be at their very best."
> —Vera Wang

Throughout her career in design, Vera has maintained her strong bond with figure skating. She loves taking her daughters to the rink, where she can pass on her enthusiasm for the sport. Ever since Vera began designing, she has created beautiful and functional costumes for elite figure skaters. Using the skater's music as her jumping-off point, Vera comes up with a unique design that enhances the skater's movement and complements the music perfectly. Vera has designed beautiful outfits for figure skating champion (and friend) Michelle Kwan. In 2009, Vera Wang was inducted into the U.S. Figure Skating Hall of Fame for her important contributions to the sport as a costume designer. At the 2010 Winter Olympics in Vancouver, Vera was thrilled to see U.S. skater Evan Lysacek win gold in the dramatic black bodysuit (adorned with a twisted, silvery snake of shiny sequins) she designed for him. Vera, who is known for her generosity, threw a big party for Evan after the win.

With her business thriving, it has been natural for Vera

Kate Hudson wearing a Vera Wang
wedding dress in the 2009 movie *Bride Wars*

Wang to turn her attention to social causes and to help those in need. Vera used her Fall 1999 fashion show as a fundraising venue to generate money for two different AIDS organizations. She was one of several high-profile American fashion designers who created $25 T-shirts for Fashion for Haiti—a group that raised money for victims of the January 2010 earthquake in Haiti.

From Vera's list of clients, it looks as if her focus is on the rich and famous, but she aspires to make her fashion affordable to all women. Vera says, "Let's be realistic, how many people are buying a $2,000 skirt? I love to design things that people can actually buy." With this in mind, she signed a business deal with Kohl's, a popularly priced department store, in 2006. She agreed to produce a line of ready-to-wear clothing costing from $20 to $200, called "Very Vera." Then, in 2007, she launched an even less expensive line called "Simply Vera" that includes clothing, accessories, towels, and bedding. In 2009, Vera launched a new, higher end label called "Lavender," featuring upscale styles available at exclusive stores, such as Holt Renfrew in Canada and Bloomingdales in the U.S.

Vera still works seventeen-hour days at an age when many are thinking of retirement. She regrets not spending more time having fun with her daughters, and says that even on vacation she's often working by the pool as her daughters swim. Being a top designer requires lots of world travel and late-night social events. Vera confesses that she sometimes sleeps in. She needs the extra energy because there are countless people who need to discuss things with her at the office, and she has many decisions to make. Sometimes, Vera says, she's perfectly happy just to stay home all day with the curtains drawn, and her laptop and TV to keep her company. Her hardworking nature doesn't keep her from delegating work, however. Vera says she has her assistant answer many of her e-mails and she tries to avoid phone calls, which she hates.

Vera attributes much of her success to her late parents. She says her mother was "her biggest champion" and credits her father for supporting her with his loving nature. Maybe it is due to her parents' strong loyalty, or perhaps to the genes passed on from her warrior ancestors—but about one thing there is no doubt. Vera Wang works hard to create her breathtakingly beautiful clothes, and she's established a style that's uniquely hers.

Zaha Hadid

Building the Unbuildable
1950 –

Zaha Hadid is fiercely devoted to architecture and design. Her admiration for forms and silhouettes is evident even in her personal style, which is bold and flamboyant. She dresses in iridescent, jewel-toned leggings, oversized tops, and dramatic, flowing capes. Nobody denies that Zaha is a woman who is always noticed in a crowd.

Even though it's true that most top architects happen to be men, Zaha intensely dislikes being referred to as a "woman architect." She finds this label patronizing. Zaha expects respect for her architectural genius, creativity, and technical mastery.

Though Zaha no longer has any relatives living in Iraq

and hasn't visited since the 1980s, her childhood home is very dear to her heart. Zaha has happy memories of her years in Iraq. Her father, Mohammed Hadid, was an important liberal politician, who served as Iraq's Minister of Finance in the late 1950s and early 1960s. As a young girl from a wealthy family, long before the war years began, Zaha attended an exclusive French Catholic school in Baghdad. She liked the stimulating classes given by experienced university professors, who were brought in by the French nuns to teach the girls. Mr. and Mrs. Hadid were firm believers in good education. When Zaha was sixteen, her parents sent her to top boarding schools in England and Switzerland. Her two brothers attended boarding school as well.

As a child, Zaha loved to draw. By the time she was eleven years old, her appreciation for art extended beyond her own pictures and art projects. On one occasion, she had a chance to look at extraordinary photographs of the Marsh Arab people in southern Iraq that moved her deeply. Her father's friend Wilfred Thesiger—a noted explorer who had spent his child-hood in North Africa—had taken the photos. Wilfred's love of the indigenous people shone through in his spectacular photo-graphs of the land and its people. Zaha was drawn into a new way of seeing the world around her. She could see in Wilfred's photos how the Marsh Arabs' houses and other buildings

Bauhaus

Bauhaus is a style of design that is characteristic of the Modern period. Bauhaus buildings are white, gray, black, or beige. They are stripped of decorative details, such as trim. The roofs are flat and the layouts are very open. Rooms are bare, with only the basic necessities. Forms are simple with clean lines. Beginning in 1919 as a school in Germany, the Bauhaus has had an enormous influence on all aspects of design, including art, architecture, interior design, and graphic design.

blended nature with form and structure. After accompanying her father on a trip to this region, Zaha became convinced that some day she would become an architect, to bring this vision to life. Recalling that important trip, Zaha explained, "The beauty of the landscape—where sand, water, reeds, birds, buildings and people all somehow flowed together—has never left me."

The Baghdad of Zaha's childhood was a city under the spell of modernity. The fashionable and wealthy of that time had a taste for new forms and designs. Zaha's family home was a Bauhaus-style house—the first in Baghdad. Zaha's mother ordered stylish 1950s furniture from Italy. None of these design details were lost on young Zaha. She took it all in, becoming increasingly aware of shapes and styles. One of her favorite things was an asymmetrical mirror in her bedroom. She later claimed that this mirror started her attraction to asymmetry in design.

Following high school, Zaha was keen to study architecture at the American University of Beirut, but architecture was part of the engineering department, and—remarkably—there wasn't a single female student enrolled. Reluctant to be the only woman in the architecture program, Zaha opted for a degree in mathematics instead. From there, she traveled to London, where she studied at the Architectural Association School of Architecture (the AA). There, Zaha made a big impression with her bold, revolutionary ideas, which set her apart from her fellow students.

In 1977, things started happening fast. Zaha earned her degree and accepted a position at a London firm called the Office of Metropolitan Architecture, which was founded by Rem Koolhaas, a cutting-edge, Dutch architect and Zaha's former teacher. Greek-born Elia Zenghelis—also a teacher at the AA—worked there as well. During these formative years, Zaha's drawing skills progressed steadily, thanks to Rem's tutoring and her hard work. Her hand-penned sketches were often commended for their precision and accuracy. In a short time, the talented Zaha became a partner at this architectural firm. Through her friendship with Rem, Zaha met Peter Rice, an engineer, who encouraged her to keep trying, even when others argued that her creative designs were impossible to build. It's often helpful for beginners to have support from a respected mentor or role model, and Peter's advice and encouragement helped Zaha believe in her abilities.

With more confidence, she worked harder to create her own leading-edge designs, and her efforts paid off. In 1979, she designed a private residence, 59 Eaton Place, London, which in 1982 earned her the highest British architectural design award—Gold Medal, Architectural Design. Zaha opened her own office in 1980, and while many of her early designs were shown in glossy architectural magazines—and achieved much acclaim—none of them were built. Nonetheless, fellow architects admired Zaha's work, with its sharp angles and unorthodox interiors.

As well as working at her firm, Zaha taught at the Architectural Association School of Architecture from 1978 until 1984 with Rem and Elia, and later independently. Somewhat disenchanted with the department on campus, Zaha craved the freedom of having her own space in a vibrant, creative district. The university went along with her wishes and Zaha established her own branch of the architecture department in a warehouse in historic Covent Garden Market in the middle of London's theater district. As well as being the best place to buy fruits, vegetables, and flowers, Covent Garden in the late 1970s had an edgy entertainment scene, featuring some of the punk and new wave artists emerging at that time.

In addition, she has held positions at other educational institutions, including Harvard, Columbia, and Yale. Designing and teaching have been the fuel that kept Zaha going. She remained single and didn't have any children. Always well dressed and stylish, she enjoys attracting a lot of attention. She is known for her charm, but she can switch it off in a second if her exacting standards are not met, unleashing her impatience on those around her. Working with a boss like this is not always easy, but at least one former employee has said that if a staffer is going through a difficult time, Zaha is the first to offer her help.

In 1983 Zaha won the competition to design The Peak, a country club in Hong Kong. (Most architectural projects are set up as a competition among firms who must create drawings and models of the proposed building. These are judged by a committee, which ultimately chooses a winner.) Even though this project was never built, from this point onward the name of Zaha Hadid began to filter into everyday conversations. She was starting to achieve celebrity status, which was just fine with her. Zaha's strong presence and charisma made people think she was a celebrity long before she became one. In some ways, it was inevitable that she attained fame. It suited her personality.

In 1993, what should have been a major opportunity turned sour. Zaha won a $49 million bid to design the Cardiff Bay Opera House in Wales. She created a remarkable, futuristic design, but rumors abounded that the design was impossible to build. In 1995, the project was killed, and a local architect was commissioned to build a more subdued and conservative opera house. After this unfortunate debacle, Zaha questioned whether or not she should keep working in the field of architecture. After a short time, she shook off the criticisms and soldiered on, refusing to let the opinions of others derail her ambitions.

Meanwhile, in 1994, Zaha designed and built the Vitra Fire Station on site at the Vitra Design Factory in Weil am Rhein, along the Rhine River. The Vitra company manufactured modern furniture by acclaimed designers, including the famous American husband-and-wife design duo Charles and Ray Eames. The Vitra Design Museum, established in 1989, attracts an international audience who come to research and view its wonderful collections of furniture, interior design, and architecture.

Although it was small, Zaha's fire-station project was important for her career. It was the first of her designs to take flight and evolve from a paper design to a real, three-dimensional structure. Moreover, this commission put Zaha on the same level as renowned architects Frank Gehry, Buckminster Fuller, and others who contributed unconventional structures to this site that showcases modern design. Zaha's fire station boasts odd angles and sharp points of concrete jutting into the air. It was rumored that the building was closed because it wasn't large enough to hold fire trucks, but this wasn't true. When a nearby fire department began to serve the area, the on-site fire station was no longer necessary. The building was retained, and transformed into a gallery that displays a vast collection of beautiful designer chairs.

Zaha continued to work on German structures for several more years. In addition to the fire station, she is celebrated for her designs of the LFone Pavilion and Land Formation-One, also situated in Weil am Rhein. Zaha was grateful for these opportunities to build.

Zaha hit a dry spell in 1996 that lasted for three years. She couldn't get any projects built or accepted. This taught her not to refuse any reasonable project offer. Eventually, she became very busy indeed. She had to increase the number of employees at her architectural firm—first to three hundred, then to four hundred.

> "I started out trying to create buildings that would sparkle like isolated jewels; now I want them to connect, to form a new kind of landscape, to flow together with contemporary cities and the lives of their peoples."
>
> –Zaha Hadid

There is only one Zaha, however, and while she doesn't always do the drawings at Zaha Hadid Architects, she is the overseeing visionary for every design.

Zaha designed the Phaeno Science Centre in Wolfsburg, Germany in 2000. The spaceship-like structure perches on concrete cones. In true Zaha-fashion the fluid lines of the building, which is made of concrete and glass, blend with the environment of the city. The construction of this building was made possible through the use of self-compacting concrete, which freely flows into forms before hardening into a smooth, durable material. At the time, this building was the largest structure in Europe to be built with this material.

Zaha's futuristic forms next appeared on the ski slopes when she designed the famous Bergisel Ski Jump in 2002. Located on Bergisel Mountain in the Austrian Alps, above the historic city of Innsbruck, the jump resembles a huge, concrete high-heeled shoe.

In 2004, Zaha won the $100,000 Pritzker Architecture Prize, an incredible achievement. In fact, she was the first woman ever to receive this prize. The Pritzker, a U.S. honor, is to architecture what the Nobel Prize is to the fields of chemistry, literature, peace, physics, physiology, and medicine. Zaha received the award for her jigsaw-like design of the Rosenthal Center for Contemporary Art in Cincinnati, Ohio, which she designed in 1998. Construction began in 2001 and finished in 2003. This corner building in an urban setting is a gorgeous assemblage of blocks of concrete, glass, and metal, stacked and cantilevered high above the streets. A Zaha-designed "Urban Carpet" connects the street to the art gallery's lobby and up to the gallery levels, located on floors two to six. The manner in which this "carpet" links each floor and curves up at the rear of the building provides a fluid connection between the outside city and the interior galleries. The zigzag "step-ramp" at the back of the building gives visitors access to the galleries and offers pleasing views both into the galleries and out onto the street. Zaha's design allows the gallery to hover between two worlds: art and society.

In 2005, Zaha won a highly competitive bid to design the massive Aquatic Centre for the London 2012 Olympics. When the Minister of Culture and Sport claimed her project had doubled in cost, Zaha wasn't going to let this comment sabotage her design and impact her career. She immediately contacted Lord Rogers, a high-profile architect, and had him write letters to the media in defense of her superb design. This time, instead of being pushed out of her own project, Zaha received a public apology, and got back to work.

Mulling over her international portfolio of unique urban structures—encompassing museums, art galleries, forums,

Zaha Hadid in front of MAXXI–Museum of Art for the XXI Century– in Rome, Italy, a building she designed.

civic centers, hotels, and sky-scrapers—Zaha feels something tugging on her social con-science. She freely admits, "What I would really love to build are schools, hospitals, social housing. Of course I believe imaginative architec-

> Zaha Hadid also designs furni-ture, and her daring designs are sought after internationally. Her "Aqua" table, with its blue top, sold for $296,000 at an auction in 2006.

ture can make a difference to people's lives, but I wish it was possible to divert some of the effort we put into ambitious museums and galleries into the basic architectural building blocks of society."

In the meantime, commissions for dramatic, large-scale structures keep her architectural firm buzzing with activity. And even medical buildings, such as Maggie's Cancer Care Centre in Fife, Scotland, take on Zaha Hadid's characteris-tic points and angles to make the building seem less like an institution. After all, why bother creating buildings destined to remain in the background? It's simply not Zaha's style.

As a gesture of goodwill, Zaha donated the design of Maggie's Centre. Since this center is also Zaha's first per-manent construction in the United Kingdom, where she now lives, it is personally meaningful for her. The beautiful, natural surroundings of the hospital complement the tranquil focus of the care center, and again demonstrate Zaha's desire to link buildings to the natural environment. It isn't as revolutionary as many of her other buildings, but it does feature a few sur-prises, including many triangular windows. Maggie's Centre took two years to construct, and opened in 2006.

An interviewer once asked Zaha how she became so successful: "Is it fate, or is it luck?" Zaha replied, "Neither! It's hard work!" Zaha continues to work hard and to push the boundaries and experiment in new areas. For the 2009 Manchester International Festival in England, she adapted her talents to create an indoor Bach Salon. Rather than representing the mood of Bach's music through art and design, Zaha focused on giving a physical form to the pure sound of Bach, while at the same time enhancing the acoustics. First, she wrapped a sinewy steel frame in a thick, winding panel of pearl-white, stretchy, Lycra, which gave structure to the empty space. Then, she enhanced the acoustics with a sail-like expanse of cloth, by stretching it into a smooth, snail-shaped spiral that looks like a magnified inner ear. This soft cocoon of intimate space, in which music lovers could listen to Bach sonatas performed live, received highly favorable reviews from visitors, art critics, and interior designers alike. The fluid, moving impression of this installation is in keeping with Zaha's use of "frozen motion" in her designs. Whether it is frozen waves, ripples of sand, or whorls on a shell, her natural motifs give the illusion of great energy and movement.

Now a self-professed Londoner, Zaha embraces the multi-cultural, cosmopolitan feel of the city. While the experimental style of her architecture often appeals to philosophical thinkers, Zaha still finds her themes solidly rooted in nature. She states, "I don't design nice buildings—I don't like them. I like architecture to have some raw, vital, earthy quality."

Zaha's daring architectural designs defy convention. They are wildly original and often described as optimistic. With her uncompromising outlook, Zaha is determined to hold fast to her creative visions, and see them through to their spectacular finish. While function is a critical element in her designs, Zaha forges forms that relate to the natural landscape, stimulate thinking, and offer surprises with their unexpected angles, materials, and views. Through the tireless efforts of one of the most powerful architects of the 21st century, the possibilities of human engineering and design have been pushed to another level altogether. Star architect Zaha Hadid has given the world a window into the way the future will look.

Aissa Dione

Celebrating Senegal Tradition
1952 –

The streets of Dakar, capital of the ancient West African nation of Senegal, are crowded all day with people going about their business, many wearing traditional robes, elegant kaftans, long dresses, or stylish head-wraps made of the bright local cotton cloth. In countless street markets and shops, tailors stand in front of tall stacks of colorful fabric, and women pause to admire new patterns that can be made up into regal, flowing garments in the Senegalese style. On the street, people speak a combination of local African languages and French— for the French were present in Senegal from the late 1600s, until the colony became independent in 1960.

Aissa Dione was born in Dakar. Her mother was French;

her father was Senegalese. She grew up in France, and earned a degree in fine arts. Her education gave her a strong technical background, which would help her out later. Aissa moved back to Dakar in her twenties with the idea that she would work as an artist. She did this happily for five years, before she found her true calling.

A chance encounter with a local art collector changed the life of the young Senegalese artist. Meeting on a busy street one day, the man asked if Aissa was still painting. She told him she still had her studio and had just given a workshop on batik art. The collector said he'd love to buy another of her pieces, but that he needed to have his office redecorated first. Looking up and squaring her shoulders, Aissa remembers that she surprised herself by saying, "You know, I'm good with colors and patterns. Why don't you hire me to decorate your office?"

The bold question hung between them for what seemed a very long time. Then the air erupted with the art patron's hearty laughter. "Of course! Why not?" He shook Aissa's slim hand and smiled broadly.

Batik

The Soninke and the Woluf tribes in Senegal are famous for their batik designs. Artisans first trace, stencil, or wood-block designs onto the plain cotton or silk, then brush melted beeswax, paraffin—or even rice paste—onto certain areas of the fabric. After the wax has dried, they dye the fabric with whatever color is the lightest. The dye seeps into every wax-free area of the cloth, and trickles into tiny cracks in the wax coating. The process is repeated for increasingly darker colors that the artists introduce to the design. To melt the wax and remove it from the cloth, the craftsperson drops the fabric into boiling water. Then, she hangs it to dry. The finished cloth features repeat patterns, crinkly lines, and bold tones. Batik has roots in the Middle East, West Africa, Turkey, India, China, and Japan.

This fateful conversation led to Aissa Dione's start in the field of interior design. She was immediately passionate about designing, and threw herself into her first venture with complete dedication. For this project, Aissa did something original and admirable—instead of using the imported European styles and furnishings that were popular, she very deliberately chose locally produced materials, fabrics, and tools. Then, she decided to hire only local trades people as well. From the very beginning, Aissa was determined to follow principles of sustainability *(see p.34)* in her new business. In the course of carrying out her design ideas, she even built a large weaving loom just for this job. The new loom was necessary to make unique fabrics in unusually large sizes. She went to great lengths in her creative approaches, even though she had no idea that this project would lead to any more work.

Interior Design

Interior design is a profession that involves planning and decorating an indoor area. Designs must suit both the function of the space and the artistic tastes of their client. Interior designers create plans and decorating ideas for indoor spaces, such as offices and homes. The overall color scheme, and the placement and style of furniture, window coverings, and lighting, are all part of the job. Community colleges and art schools offer diploma and degree programs in this creative field.

Finding inspiration in the rich indigenous culture and textile heritage of Senegal, Aissa used her fine-tuned sense of aesthetics to integrate traditional weaving and decorative motifs into a stylish, functional, organized, and comfortable workspace. Soon, her vision started catching on; more clients came calling. When the media got wind of her designing success, making use of traditional patterns, and—better still—using local materials and the skills of local people, they were quick to spread the word. Senegal's newspapers, radio stations, television programs, and magazines began featuring stories about this young textile designer and entrepreneur. Her pioneering ideas even started promoting Senegal's cotton to the international market in fresh new ways—and Senegalese cotton is among the best produced in the world.

One of the changes Aissa made to traditional methods of weaving fabric was to mix cotton with a fiber called raffia, which comes from a palm tree. Raffia is soft but strong, and is easy to weave with other fibers. In her experiments with new combinations of fibers, Aissa also mixed cotton with silk. Both of these new blends resulted in more durable cotton-based fabrics, which were perfectly suited for upholstery and cushions. They didn't pill up into fuzzy balls on the surface, or fray and wear out quickly, like plain cotton fabrics.

Another of Aissa's innovations had to do with the size of the woven fabric. While traditional pieces of cloth are designed to be 90 cm wide, Aissa had the idea to enlarge the loom, in order to create really impressive 140-cm-wide pieces of fabric.

African Symbols: The Comb

A traditional design Aissa admires and often uses is a repeat pattern of wooden combs. A comb, or *duafe*, was a prized object used by women of the Mandjak and Akan tribes to comb and plait their hair. The wooden comb is often used as a decorative motif. It is a female symbol, which is connected to mermaids, who comb their long reed-like tresses. It was traditional for a young man to carve a beautiful wooden comb, and give it to a special woman as a token of his love for her. It is also a symbol of magic, beauty, cleanliness, and protection. According to African folktales, a hero can throw a magic comb down in the path of a pursuer. The comb transforms into a thick forest that slows the evil attacker, so that the hero can escape.

The wooden comb is also used to mark lines that will be printed on fabric. This gives the comb an even richer connection to the textile industry.

She did this to make the patterns she adapted from local traditions clearer, bolder, and more contemporary.

In Senegal, men traditionally performed the art of weaving. There were very few women weavers or textile workers. Because of that, Aissa didn't have a female mentor or role model to help her get started. When she took on her early jobs, Aissa didn't know anything about how to run a business, either. She recalls, "At that time I didn't even know how to do an invoice. I was asking friends for advice." There's nothing like learning on the job, however, and so—through trial and error—Aissa gradually added business skills to her natural artistic talents.

With her keen social conscience, Aissa was excited by the ways her company could improve the local economy and create jobs. She was also pleased that her textiles and furnishings could showcase Senegalese art and culture in Europe and North America. In the past, Senegal had exported the raw materials that it cultivated, such as cotton. Now, Aissa's business was selling home-furnishing products that were grown, dyed, woven, and sewn by Senegalese workers. "This is both good for my business and for the region," Aissa explained. "Africa can do more than simply send its raw goods overseas."

In the early 1990s, an airline inflight magazine featured a story about Aissa's woven fabrics and unique pieces for home décor. A well-known European designer read the article on a business trip. Once settled back in the office, the designer picked up the phone and placed an order for some of Aissa's fabric. The haute-couture designer loved the look and feel of the fabric, and spread the word through the design community. Soon, more orders began coming in from other European designers. Aissa was excited by the response, and, with all these orders in hand, felt it was time to register her textile design business. She named it Aissa Dione Tissus, and it was officially launched in 1992. (*Tissus* means fabrics or textiles in French.)

At Aissa's company, employees—many of whom are women—work with textiles in many different ways. Some dye, some weave, others embroider designs onto fabric, and still others sew fabric into decorative items, such as cushions, handbags, luggage, and bed covers. With the same beautiful woven fabrics, Aissa now even makes shoes. Another branch of her company makes furniture, such as armchairs, small, elegant couches or padded benches, and footstools and low, upholstered tables, which are covered in her specially designed, traditional fabrics.

The work at Aissa Dione Tissus is labor intensive, and

Aissa Dione winds a vegetable-dyed silk to add to the pile of dyed yarns on her desk in Dakar, Senegal.

the workload changes week by week. One week Aissa may have a huge order from a Paris designer. The order must be filled, and she absolutely can't be late. But the Senegalese government has strict rules about overtime hours, beyond a normal, forty-hour work week. For Aissa, this means a lot of extra paperwork to fill out, and this takes

> "No one had used [African] weaving for interior design because people did not think interior design was something that could be done in Africa."
>
> —Aissa Dione

her away from designing. According to the law, she has to pay her employees an extra 14 to 40 percent for overtime hours on weekdays or Saturdays, and over 50 percent more for overtime on Sundays or holidays. In addition to overtime challenges, it has been difficult for Aissa to get bank loans. Sometimes, she has had to turn down a large order simply because she didn't have enough cash available to buy supplies and to pay her workers. These government rules and banking limits make it very difficult to run a mid-sized textile business in Senegal—but Aissa forges ahead.

As her business was getting established, Aissa made a smart decision. She focused on the lucrative, high-end design market in Paris. Because she was raised in France, and speaks excellent French, this was a logical place for her to start finding clients. This plan worked out very well for her, and Aissa now supplies fabric to Hermes, Fendi, Christian Liaigre, and other famous fashion design houses. In addition to Paris, she exports to Italy, South Africa, and New York. When the Africa Growth and Opportunity Act was passed in 2000, African clothing and textiles could be exported into the United States without having duty (an additional tax) placed on them. This made it appealing and financially worthwhile to seek American clients, as well.

On the continent of Africa, women frequently have more

difficulties than men finding and keeping paid employment. It is more usual for women to stay home raising children and caring for their family. Household chores can take a lot of time, especially in rural areas or very poor regions. There, many women spend much of the day cooking meals, cleaning, doing laundry, growing vegetables, sewing clothes, and even finding firewood. In urban centers, more women are beginning to work as sales clerks, administrative assistants, cleaning staff, and factory workers. Needless to say, there still are not very many businesswomen or female entrepreneurs. In 2008, the World Bank presented a report on women entrepreneurs in Africa that examined the challenges these business owners face. This study was undertaken to help further the employment and strengthen the rights of women in developing countries.

As one of the few women to own and run a business in Africa, Aissa employs mostly women. Her company has an excellent reputation, and demand for its creations has been growing steadily. If she could accept all the order requests that come in, she could boost production to a staggering four times what it is now. To do this, however, she would have to hire many more workers, and this is where things get difficult. If there is a temporary drop in demand—which happens

The National Federation of Professional Apparel is an organization that supports tailors, weavers, designers, pattern makers, and dyers in Senegal. In 1999, this federation set up a wonderful training center for garment workers, with technical assistance from a group in Paris. Local companies donated much-needed sewing machines for the initiative. The Senegalese government chose a small number of students for the program and paid for their education. Clothing and textile manufacturers in Senegal knew this program could not solve all the problems that challenge them, but it was definitely a step in the right direction for this young local industry.

frequently—Aissa would have to keep paying a larger staff and would have a lot of trouble if, at some point, she needed to lay off some employees, even temporarily. "People can sue you and say you have fired them illegally," explains Aissa. To lay off a worker, the business owner must give the employee a letter stating the situation. Next, the owner must write several letters to the labor inspector, with detailed reasons for the dismissal, proof that the industry is faltering (difficult to do in the textile industry, which doesn't keep consistent statistics), and proof that she has tried other courses of action. Furthermore, business owners have no say about whom they can lay off; the order follows strict rules based on seniority, not skills or performance. "Worker protections are important," Aissa says, and she believes strongly that they should be upheld. "But," she adds with seriousness, "if they are not designed to take into account employer needs, ironically many more would-be employees suffer." The way forward is not smooth for a company like hers, with its unpredictable swings in demand.

Through hard work, sound technical skills, and a clear creative vision, Aissa has managed to build up a successful design company, despite the many challenges that face small and mid-sized businesses in Senegal. She is always on the lookout for programs and grants that can benefit her company. For example, the Ministry of Women's Entrepreneurship in Senegal offers low-interest loans to women entrepreneurs. Through this program, Aissa has secured small loans to help her company out of difficult financial situations.

Aissa's early experience as a batik artist provided her with hands-on experience in dyeing fabrics. As her artistic skills developed, she took big chances, learned new skills on the fly, and started a company that has become a shining international success. Her passion for creating simple patterns and images became the basis for her renowned, sophisticated textiles. She has had exhibitions of her work in Europe and in 1992 she won the UNESCO Prize for Africa, which honored her contemporary hand-woven fabrics.

Today, Aissa continues to gain recognition as a leader in textile design. She is paving the way for the next generation of brilliant women designers both in Senegal and throughout Africa.

Cynthia Breazeal

Friendly Robots
1967 –

Robots are great toys. You may have played with wind-up robots, traded Transformers, fed your virtual pet, or used a science kit to build a pop can "robug". But robots can be much more than playthings. For instance, scientists and engineers have started creating robots that train doctors during practice operations before surgeons try the real thing on live patients. The six-dimensional, robotic Canadarm skillfully repairs devices on the International Space Station; it bends and stretches even better than a human arm, and can lift an astounding thirty tons in zero-gravity environments. Robots smoothly construct cars on assembly lines in factories. The biggest robot surprise of all, however, is a cute, furry invention called Leonardo. Part toy, part machine, part creature, Leonardo is a "social robot" who can smile, talk, and recognize familiar faces. And he was created by innovative robot designer Cynthia Breazeal. Her robots have red lips, eyelashes, and expressive faces. Amazingly, these robots seem to feel emotion in a human-like way. Sweet? Creepy? Interesting? This dynamic designer is shaking up our perceptions about robot design, taking the term "user friendly" to a whole new level.

From a young age, Cynthia Lynn Breazeal (pronounced like Brazil) knew science and technology were in her future. Cynthia's mom was a computer scientist, and her dad was a mathematician. This was a family whose lively dinnertime conversations often centered on science.

Born in Albuquerque, New Mexico, in the American Southwest, she was raised near the technology hub in California called Silicon Valley. Cynthia was an active kid. She loved climbing trees, track and field, swimming, soccer, and tennis. When Cynthia was in grade school, she was inspired by her family's pet rat to dream of becoming a veterinarian. At the age of ten, she saw the movie *Star Wars*. It left a lasting impression. "I just fell in love with the Droids," she recounts. "But I was old enough to realize those kinds of robots didn't exist." She loved the way the film's robot characters R2-D2 and C-3P0 were "more like friends." Cynthia continues, "We cared about them and they cared about us."

In grade five or six, young Cynthia wrote a story about a robot. The last sentence of the story was "And its feelings run on a computer." How's that for foreshadowing the future? In high school, she focused on tennis and soccer. Little did she know then that the team spirit and determination she gained from playing sports would help her meet the challenges of graduate school—and long hours in the lab. For a while, she thought she'd be a medical doctor, but her parents encouraged her to pursue engineering, and to keep her options open. Later, she set her sights on space travel, and in order to become a mission specialist—like astronaut Julie Payette—Cynthia thought about studying astronomy.

After high school, Cynthia headed to the University of California, Santa Barbara. She graduated in 1989—aged twenty-one—with a major in electrical and computer engineering. Next, she went to the Massachusetts Institute of Technology (MIT), where she joined its world-renowned robotics laboratory. Cynthia's academic advisor was Dr. Rodney Brooks—a big name in the field of artificial intelligence (AI). Three years later, Cynthia earned a Masters of Science. As a graduate student and member of the MIT's AI Lab, she became a leading designer for Cog, a six-foot tall robot. The AI Lab team completed Cog in 1997. Right after that, Cynthia spearheaded work on the robotic head called Kismet. She wanted to design a social robot that people would enjoy and focused her research on the ways people interact with robots. She gathered all of her observations, findings, and discoveries, and wrote a doctoral dissertation called "Sociable Machines: Expressive Social Exchange Between Humans and Robots." Based on the value of this insightful paper, Cynthia earned her doctorate at MIT in 2000.

While working as a grad student in MIT's AI Lab, Cynthia began to develop her own ideas about robots and humans. She became interested in robots that "help us live more enriching lives." Rather than work on robots that replace humans in the workplace, which had already been done, Cynthia wanted to invent robots that would work cooperatively with people in a pleasing manner. For example, Cynthia believed robot companions could help elderly people live independently for longer by lending a hand with cooking meals—without taking over completely. The robot might remove tight-fitting lids from jars, help with chopping, and make sure the oven wasn't left on afterwards. In this way, senior citizens could

Cynthia loves to read. When she's not reading academic journals and scholarly books, she relaxes with a science fiction novel. Cynthia's always analyzing the fictional robots' character traits, and making comparisons. She notes, "We have a lot of suspicion of robots in the West. But if you look cross-culturally, that isn't true. In Japan, in their science fiction, robots are seen as good. They have Astro Boy, this character they've fallen in love with and he's fundamentally good; always there to help people."

enjoy a better quality of life, while still making choices and staying active. Cynthia began working toward bringing robots into the lives of everyday people in ways that complement, support, and enrich. These ideas, which started in graduate school, are still the heart and soul of her work today.

When Cynthia talks about human-robot communication, she often uses pets as an example to explain her ideas clearly. She points out that while using voice commands with their dogs, people instinctively talk to their pet in a high-pitched voice to show they are pleased with the dog. Similarly, using a low-pitched voice signals disapproval of the dog's behavior. These commands are effective, and they also strengthen the bond between pet owner and pet. Cynthia explains, "Even though your dog is not human, it doesn't mean you can't communicate with it in a human-like way." Applying this kind of thinking to robots is a huge change from the way we've interacted with machines up to now. Social robots that exhibit human-like emotions and characteristics blur the boundaries between humans and machines. It's a completely new frontier.

Back in the AI Lab, when her Kismet robot was fully functional, Cynthia took lots of notes as visitors began to see what it could do. She didn't just observe Kismet; she also watched how people reacted to the socially expressive machine that could smile and frown, look surprised, and pull away. "I would

much rather build something and interact with it than phi-
losophize about it," remarked Cynthia. Kismet was designed
as an eight-pound head and neck. Cynthia and the other
designers put a lot of energy into the look and movement of
Kismet's facial features. The design team consulted with a
special-effects expert to give the head human characteristics;
eyes, eyebrows, eyelids, a mouth, and ears. Cynthia and her
team programmed Kismet with fifteen computers to recognize
people's faces by analyzing different skin tones and the characteristics of people's eyes. The programmers also designed

Cynthia Breazeal's robot called Kismet—
kismet is Turkish for "fate" or "destiny".

103

the robot to be attracted to colorful objects, such as toys and puppets.

Twenty-one motors, four cameras, and a microphone enable Kismet to move, bend, react, "hear," and "see" in a convincing way. To show sadness, its red mouth turns down and it lowers its eyes. To show surprise, Kismet raises its fuzzy eyebrows, opens its mouth, and perks up its ears. Just like a baby or a toddler, if something or someone startles Kismet, the robot pulls back and appears to guard its personal space. Kismet is also programmed to learn from its interactions—through artificial intelligence.

Cynthia designed Kismet to make eye contact with people. If a person moves to another chair, Kismet's head turns, and its gaze remains trained on the person. This makes people feel closer to Kismet because the robot appears to give them its full attention. All of these qualities result in a social robot that is known for charming people. (Kismet can wink, too.) It's not unusual for people to give Kismet gifts and be rewarded with a big smile. On the other hand, when too much is happening at the same time, Kismet slows down, looks tired, gets quiet, closes its big blue eyes, and falls asleep. It seems even robots need a break sometimes. Learning is hard work!

When Cynthia heard Kismet's first, very own, original (not programmed) words "[|][ch'ao<186>][el'ao<139>z] ['aa<138>rr<109>]," she was delighted and proud. Even though the words were gibberish to humans, they showed that Kismet was acquiring new knowledge from its environment. With more learning, Kismet's human speech could improve, too.

Cynthia bid good-bye to Kismet and Cog when MIT hired her as a professor shortly after she received her doctorate. She founded the Personal Robots Group at MIT's Media Lab in 2001. Working as director of this center, Cynthia continued to pursue her robot dreams.

That same year, Cynthia had the good fortune to meet

film director Steven Spielberg—famous for directing *Jurassic Park, E.T.: The Extra Terrestrial, Raiders of the Lost Ark,* and *Close Encounters of the Third Kind.* He was making *Artificial Intelligence: A.I.* and had some questions about artificial intelligence. Cynthia was happy to fill him in. Through helping with *A.I.,* Cynthia met Stan Winston of Stan Winston Studio. Winston is a famous Hollywood mechanized creature designer who created the special effects for *Avatar* and *Iron Man,* and designed the robots for the *Terminator* films. When Cynthia and her team from the Personal Robots Group at MIT began to design their first robot, they collaborated with Stan Winston Studio from the start. The studio's expertise in animation and puppet design was exactly what the team wanted for the next social robot. "We're trying to build a creature," Cynthia explained. "We're not trying to build just a robot demo program. We're trying to build a robotic creature." Stan's team named the robot Leonardo after one of the most accomplished and well-rounded people of all time—Leonardo da Vinci, the extraordinarily talented sculptor, painter, inventor, and scientist who lived in Italy during the Renaissance. Cynthia was thrilled with the name not only because Leonardo da Vinci is one of her heroes, but also because her robot would have characteristics that came from both art and science.

The first working prototype was a big hit. Leonardo was furry, cute, and charismatic. He was two-and-a-half feet tall

On Girls Pursuing Science

"Girls aren't discouraged, but they aren't encouraged either."

"I am a woman, but it's also that I was raised the way I was raised, at the time I was raised. I, as a whole package, bring these insights. I can't just describe it to you by gender or the fact that I was raised in California or that my parents were scientists. I can't say here's the one thing. It's all of those things."

—Cynthia Breazeal

Cynthia has been interested in the ways parents interact with infants and toddlers since she was a graduate student. She applied theories and knowledge from early childhood psychology to design Kismet and Leonardo. Now that she's a parent, Cynthia pays close attention to the ways in which Ryan and Nathan learn. Cynthia's first-hand observations could be incorporated into her next generation of sophisticated social robots.

and had more than sixty motors that were programmed to produce a full range of gestures and movements—including shrugging shoulders, pointing, and looking at an object.

Cynthia led her team of designers, researchers, and technicians to conduct studies with their creation. People worked one-on-one with Leonardo, teaching it to manipulate objects. Through artificial intelligence, Leonardo learned how to do simple tasks, such as pushing the correct color of button when asked. Leo is an incredible machine with the ability to learn from humans in the same ways that people learn from each other—not in computer programming language. "The fact that it's a machine melts away when you begin to interact with it," Cynthia explains. "Maybe someday it will be a genuine creature in its own right."

Cynthia married MIT graduate Robert (Bobby) Blumofe in 2003. After working as associate professor of computer science at the University of Texas, Bobby joined a technology firm, where he holds an executive position in Networks and Operations. Cynthia and Bobby have two boys: Ryan and Nathan.

Wired magazine ranked Leo among "The 50 Best Robots Ever" in 2006. Cynthia talks about her creation with great pride: "Leonardo is, I would say, the most sophisticated social robot...the most expressive robot in the world today."

Never one to sit back and take a break, Cynthia is still striving to improve Leonardo by fine-tuning her design. A new hand prototype with built-in touch sensors, achieved through layering silicone materials, is being developed to heighten the robot's perception of touch. (Silicone materials are used for special effects in the film industry, and Stan Winston Studio has a big role in this development as well.) Eventually, the design team wants to give Leo all-over touch-sensing abilities, so that he can distinguish pleasure from pain. Maybe he'll even be ticklish.

Becoming a mother made Cynthia more aware of toys for babies and toddlers, and this got her brainstorming new ideas. What if she could develop a robotic teddy bear that would comfort toddlers who were in hospital? Young children who have to brave a night away from their loved ones, surrounded by unfamiliar sights and sounds, are often overwhelmed by fear and loneliness. But if these young patients had an extra special bear, their hospital stay could be less traumatic. Cynthia and her team at the Personal Robots Group got to work on creating a cuddly, plush toy with robotic features that could help take away the sting of separations from parents and grandparents. Studies show that petting a dog can lower people's blood pressure, and pets in nursing homes can make elderly residents feel happier. Cynthia's team believes their innovative toy will have similar benefits for children.

"Appreciate that those [grade-school math and science] skills are so powerful. They allow you to create and think about things with tremendous creative empowerment. So whether you apply that to traditional science or whether you apply that to do special effects in films or to go to Mars or whatever—all of those skills keep building on each other all the way through college and beyond. If you really want the kind of job where you get to decide what you want to build, what you want to do, what you want to achieve, you have that creative freedom. Science and technology is a great field to pursue to allow you to do that."

—Cynthia Breazeal

Cynthia Breazeal's robotic flower sways when touched by human hands.

Called the Huggable, this new interactive robot is designed for use in health-care and education, but also enhances social communication with absent loved ones. More than 1,500 skin sensors enable the robot to "feel" hugs and record the child's temperature. The mechanical systems are buried within the soft, lifelike, silicone-skinned plush toy so that its gears are soundless and hidden. Cameras in the eyes and microphones in the ears facilitate communication with a "remote operator" (the far-away parent or grandparent) through a web interface. By logging onto a website, the parent or caregiver can type in text, which the teddy bear can then say aloud to the child. The Huggable's microphone picks up the child's voice, and the system is designed to transmit the voice to the parent or caregiver through the website. The "whole-body gesture recognition" ability tells the parent or nurse what the child is doing to the bear—picking it up, rocking it, bouncing it, or throwing it. In situations where seriously ill children cannot have any visitors due to their medical conditions, the robot allows communication without a tangle of wires and cords. Cynthia says, "Being a parent has certainly influenced my work...to try to make a more direct connection between my academic life and helping real people."

> For young people who are considering a career in robotics, Cynthia recommends studying computer science and taking some courses in artificial intelligence, psychology, electronics, and mechanical design.

Cynthia Breazeal is a revolutionary designer in the field of social robotics. Her passion for robots that interact with people in human ways has changed the way we view robotic machines. By holding fast to her leading-edge ideas, and working with a team of skilled robot and special effect experts, Cynthia continues to surprise the world with her imaginative, endearing, visually pleasing, and functionally useful robotic creatures. One of her latest creations is Nexi, "a mobile, dexterous, social robot" that has the ability to find victims in burning buildings or hazardous areas and lead them to safety. If Cynthia's dream goes as planned, her groundbreaking social robots may become commonplace in the not-so-distant future. Ready for one in your life?

Sources & Resources

* for children

Eileen Gray

Adam, Peter. *Eileen Gray: Architect/Designer: a Biography*. Rev. ed. New York: Harry N. Abrams, 2000.

ArchiSeek: Ireland—Eileen Gray
http://ireland.archiseek.com/tesserae/000007.html

Colley, Kelly. "Eileen Gray Finally Gets Her Due" http://www.metrop-olismag.com/pov/20090716/eileen-gray-finally-gets-her-due

Design Within Reach: Eileen Gray
http://www.dwr.com/category/designers/d-g/eileen-gray.do

"Eileen Gray: Architect + Furniture Designer"
http://designmuseum.org/design/eileen-gray

Eileen (Kathleen) (Moray) Gray
http://eng.archinform.net/arch/3038.htm

McDermott, Catherine. *Design Museum Book of Twentieth-Century Design*. London, UK: Carlton Books, 1997.

Jane Jacobs

Allen, Max, ed., *Ideas That Matter: The Worlds of Jane Jacobs.* Owen Sound, ON: The Ginger Press, 1997.

An Urban Visionary
http://www.canada.com/vancouversun/voices/story.html?id=2b2816da-43c3-4237-a572-3356a4747a81&p=1

Biography of Jane Jacobs
http://bss.sfsu.edu/pamuk/urban/bio.html

Jacobs, Jane. *The Death and Life of Great American Cities.* New York, NY: Random House, 1961.

Jane Jacobs
http://www.pps.org/info/placemakingtools/placemakers/jjacobs

Jane Jacobs
http://www.notablebiographies.com/supp/Supplement-Fl-Ka/Jacobs-Jane.html

Jane Jacobs Bio
http://www.thinkcity.ca/node/60

Jane Jacobs Biography
http://www.biography.com/articles/Jane-Jacobs-9351679

Jane Jacobs Biography
http://www.biographybase.com/biography/Jacobs_Jane.html

The Triumph of Jane Jacobs
http://www.nysun.com/arts/triumph-of-jane-jacobs/63089/

Cornelia Hahn Oberlander

Aird, Louise, "Arthur Erickson & Cornelia Oberlander: The 'A' Team of Canadian Landscape Architecture," *Landscape Trades*. June 1994.

Beyond the Garden: Landscape Architect Cornelia Hahn Oberlander Discusses Her Ahead-of-the-Curve Career in Sustainability
http://www.metropolismag.com/story/20070613/beyond-the-garden

Chung, Susan Ng, "Sustainable Design Ideas Fair," *Canadian Teacher Magazine*. September 2009, pp. 8, 9.

Cornelia
http://www.aibc.ca/pram/interviews/cornelia.html

Cornelia Hahn Oberlander
http://www.theflowerexpert.com/content/flowerexperts/
cornelia-hahn-oberlander

Cornelia Hahn Oberlander Archive
http://www.cca.qc.ca/en/collection/453-cornelia-hahn-oberlander-
archive

Cornelia Oberlander
http://www.corneliaoberlander.ca/

Design Intelligence—Excerpt of Pioneers: Cornelia Oberlander Interview (video)
http://www.di.net/videos/3018/

Garden in the Sky
http://www2.canada.com/vancouvercourier/news/story.
html?id=3e5dc38b-e69e-48bf-92bb-af4383527a5b&p=3

Hall, Jenny. "A Pioneer with an Eye for Invention," *Smith Alumnae Quarterly*. Fall 2004.

Scott, Sarah, "Queen of Green," *Canadian Geographic*. September/ October, 2007, pp. 87 – 90.

* Stinson, Kathy. *Love Every Leaf: The Life of Landscape Architect Cornelia Hahn Oberlander*. Toronto, ON: Tundra Books, 2008.

Taylor, Timothy. "Mother Nature," *Vancouver*. Jan./Feb. 2007.

Suzanne E. Vanderbilt

Automotive Design Oral History Project: The Reminiscences of Suzanne E. Vanderbilt
http://www.autolife.umd.umich.edu/Design/Vanderbilt/Vanderbiltinterview.htm

Damsels of Design
http://www.core77.com/awid/damsels.html

Gordy, Cynthia. "Designing Woman" *Essence*. Sept. 2007, vol. 38, issue 5, p. 130.

Kelly, Kevin M. "Denise Gray: Electrifying GM's Future" *Automotive Design & Production*. Nov. 2008, vol. 120, issue 11, p. 20.

McAvoy, Linda. "Car Buyers Benefit from Women's Input" *The Toronto Star*. Sat., Nov. 9, 2002, p. G-12.

Suzanne E. Vanderbilt http://www.autolife.umd.umich.edu/Design/Vanderbilt/Vanderbilt.html

Suzanne Vanderbilt's Inflatable Back Support
http://www.autolife.umd.umich.edu/Design/Vanderbilt/Back_Support.htm

World's Automotive Design Legacy: Automotive Hollywood—The Battle for Body Beautiful
http://www.carofthecentury.com/designing_women.htm

Eiko Ishioka

Art Directors Club: 1992 Hall of Fame—Eiko Ishioka
http://www.adcglobal.org/archive/hof/1992/?id=217

Cirque du Soleil: Varekai—Press Kit
http://www.cirquedusoleil.com/en/~/media/press/PDF/varekai/
presskitvarekai.pdf

Creators: Eiko Ishioka—Costume Designer
http://www.cirquedusoleil.com/en/shows/varekai/show/creators/
eiko-ishioka.aspx

Eiko Ishioka communicates in taffeta and lace
http://libraridan.wordpress.com/2008/03/18/eiko-ishioka-
communicates-in-taffeta-and-lace/

Eiko Ishioka Interview
http://community.livejournal.com/eiko_ishioka

Friede, Eva. "Cirque Couture: Designer juggles function, form and
fantasy." *The Gazette*. Apr. 23, 2002. p. F-1.

Graphics Interview: Eiko Ishioka by Linda Cooper
http://findarticles.com/p/articles/mi_qa3992/is_200011/
ai_n8916895/?tag=content;col1

Ishioka, Eiko. *Eiko by Eiko: Eiko Ishioka, Japan's Ultimate Designer*.
San Francisco, CA: Chronicle Books, 1990.

Ishioka, Eiko. *Eiko On Stage*. New York, NY: Callaway, 2000.

Joseph, Joe. "Land where a daughter has also risen" *The Times*.
London, England. Nov. 16, 1990.

Maggie Text: 12 Japanese Masters
http://www.maggietext.com/books/12jm/index.html

Starkman, Randy and Jim Byers. "Holy aerodynamic styling—Olympic superheroes!; Futuristic suits should give athletes extra zip at Salt Lake." *Toronto Star.* Jan. 22, 2002. p. E-1.

Thomas, Kevin. "'Mishima' is a designer's delight." *Los Angeles Times.* 24 Oct., 1985, p. 1.

Ritu Kumar

Costumes and Textiles of Royal India: Ritu Kumar
http://nirmalamagazine.wordpress.com/2008/06/07/costumes-and-textiles-of-royal-india-ritu-kumar/

Designer Ritu Kumar raises a toast to today's woman
http://www.dnaindia.com/entertainment/report_designer-ritu-kumar-raises-a-toast-to-today-s-woman_1363166

Indian Designer—Ritu Kumar
http://www.scribd.com/doc/3378292/Indian-Fashion-Designer-Ritu-Kumar

Indian fashion industry is still very young, says Ritu Kumar
http://www.encyclopedia.com/doc/1P3-1243732561.html

Kumar, Ritu; Cathy Muscat, editor. *Costumes and Textiles of Royal India.* Suffolk, UK: Antique Collectors' Club, 2000.

Ritu Kumar
http://www.ritukumar.com

Ritu Kumar
http://www.mapsofindia.com/who-is-who/health-life-style/ritu-kumar.html

Ritu Kumar Bridal Collection
http://sareez.wordpress.com/2010/03/13/ritu-kumar-bridal-collection/

Ritu Kumar Collection
http://www.ritukumar.org/

Ritu Kumar Special
http://www.shaadionline.com/ritu-kumar.asp

Trebay, Guy. "More Is More, With a Dollop of Too Much," *New York Times*: May 5, 2005; p. G-1.

Trebay, Guy. "Fashion from India, Beyond the Bangles," *New York Times*: May 13, 2003; p. B-11.

Vera Wang

Biography: Vera Wang
http://www.answers.com/topic/vera-wang

New York Fashion: Vera Wang
http://nymag.com/fashion/fashionshows/designers/bios/verawang/

The Unbridled Entrepreneur: The Early Years of Vera Wang
http://www.evancarmichael.com/Famous-Entrepreneurs/3202/The-Unbridled-Entrepreneur-The-Early-Years-of-Vera-Wang.html

Vera Wang
http://www.verawangonweddings.com/

Vera Wang Biography
http://www.biography.com/articles/Vera-Wang-9542398

Vera Wang Biography
http://www.thebiographychannel.co.uk/biographies/vera-wang.html

Vera Wang Biography
http://www.biographybase.com/biography/Wang_Vera.html

Vera Wang Bridal House Ltd.
http://www.referenceforbusiness.com/businesses/M-Z/Vera-Wang-Bridal-House-Ltd.html

Vera Wang: Dresses
http://verawang.me/quotes

Vera Wang's Second Honeymoon
http://nymag.com/nymetro/news/people/features/15541/

The 100 Most Inspiring Asian Americans of All Time: Vera Wang
http://www.goldsea.com/Personalities/Inspiring/wangv.html

Vera Wang: The Workhorse
http://www.goldsea.com/Personalities/Ox/wang.html

Vera Wang on Weddings
http://www.verawangonweddings.com/fashion/Fashion.aspx

* Louie, Ai-Ling; illustrated by Cathy Peng. *Vera Wang: Queen of Fashion, Amazing Asian American.* North Branch, NJ: Dragoneagle Press, 2007.

Who Is Vera Wang?
http://weddings.about.com/od/styleandattire/a/VeraWang.htm?p=1

Who's Who—Designers: Vera Wang
http://www.infomat.com/whoswho/verawang.html

Zaha Hadid
#69 Zaha Hadid
http://www.forbes.com/lists/2008/11/biz_powerwomen08_Zaha-Hadid_VB2V_print.html

Architect who has built a reputation for controversy
http://www.timesonline.co.uk/tol/sport/olympics/london_2012/article598479.ece

For ever thinking outside the boxy
http://entertainment.timesonline.co.uk/tol/arts_and_entertainment/visual_arts/article1988806.ece

Guest Editor: Zaha Hadid
http://news.bbc.co.uk/today/hi/today/newsid_7785000/7785759.stm

'I don't do nice'
http://www.guardian.co.uk/artanddesign/2006/oct/09/architecture.communities

Seabrook, John. "The Abstractionist." *The New Yorker.* New York, NY Dec. 21, 2009, p. 113.

Terminal Hoenheim Nord: Zaha Hadid
http://www.mimoa.eu/projects/France/Hoenheim/Terminal%20Hoenheim%20Nord

Zaha Hadid
http://www.zaha-hadid.com/

Zaha Hadid
http://www.guardian.co.uk/lifeandstyle/2008/mar/09/women.architecture

Zaha Hadid: A Diva for the Digital Age
http://www.nytimes.com/2006/06/02/arts/design/02hadi.html

Zaha Hadid's Bach salon
http://www.guardian.co.uk/artanddesign/2009/jul/01/zaha-hadid-bach-salon-architecture

Zaha Hadid: Opere e Progetti
http://www.darc.beniculturali.it/zaha_hadid/index_en.html

The New York Times: Zaha Hadid
http://www.nytimes.com/slideshow/2008/01/23/arts/20080123_HADID_SLIDESHOW_index.html

Aissa Dione

Aissa Dione
http://www.aissadionetissus.com/

Aissa Dione Textiles
http://www.africa-now.org/resources/storycards/Aissa%20Dione%20Textiles.pdf

Creating Jobs through Art
http://www.doingbusiness.org/documents/Women_in_Africa-
AissaDionne.pdf

Creative Craftsworkers: UNESCO Crafts Prize 1990 - 1995
http://unesdoc.unesco.org/images/0011/001180/118071eb.pdf

Easing Restrictions on Fixed-term Contracts—a Popular Reform
Feature in 2007/08
http://www.doingbusiness.org/documents/fullreport/2009/
Employing_Workers.pdf

IFC-World Bank Report Promotes Reforms for Women's
Entrepreneurship in Africa
http://www.ifc.org/ifcext/media.nsf/content/SelectedPressRelease?
OpenDocument&UNID=61DCF9B5FCB9E04C852574280072CBB7

Obstacles and Opportunities for Senegal's International
Competitiveness
http://www.worldbank.org/afr/wps/wp37.pdf

Pattern & Texture by Essence
http://patternandtexturebyessence.blogspot.com/2009/08/aissa-
dionne.html

Senegal Artisan Directory
https://www.onudi.org.ar/fileadmin/user_media/Services/PSD/
Clusters_and_Networks/Senegal_Artisan_Directory.pdf

Senegal: Aissa Dione Tissus
http://www.designafrica.ca/profile.php?uId=16

Cynthia Breazeal

* Brown, Jordan D. *Robo World: The Story of Robot Designer Cynthia Breazeal.* Women's Adventures in Science series. Washington, D.C.: Joseph Henry Press, 2006.

Computing (pp. 60, 62)
http://ai.stanford.edu/~serafim/mitComputing.pdf

Cynthia Breazeal by Adam Cohen (Time)
http://www.time.com/time/magazine/article/
0,9171,1101001204-90515,00.html

* Cynthia Breazeal—The Robot Designer (audio and video)
http://www.iwaswondering.org/cynthia_homepage.html

Dr. Cynthia Breazeal
http://web.media.mit.edu/~cynthiab/

Dr. Cynthia Breazeal
http://robotic.media.mit.edu/people/cynthia/cynthia.html

Dr. Cynthia Breazeal—Biography
http://web.media.mit.edu/~cynthiab/bio/bio.html

Glick, Jon. "A Conversation with Cynthia Breazeal: A Passion to Build a Better Robot, One with Social Skills and a Smile." *AI Magazine* 25.3 (2004): 96.

Meet Kismet
http://www.robotbooks.com/kismet-robot.htm

* Nova Science Now—Profile: Cynthia Breazeal (Videos)
http://www.pbs.org/wgbh/nova/sciencenow/3318/03.html

Nova Science Now: November 21, 2006 (Profile: Cynthia Breazeal)—Transcripts
http://www.pbs.org/wgbh/nova/transcripts/3318_sciencen.html

Personal Robots Group: Leonardo
http://robotic.media.mit.edu/projects/robots/leonardo/overview/overview.html

* Robot Pals: A Conversation with Cynthia Breazeal
http://www.pbs.org/saf/1510/features/breazeal.htm

* Editor of Yes Mag. *Robots: From Everyday to Out of This World.* Kids Can Press, 2008.

Talking Robots: Cynthia Breazeal—Personal Robots
http://lis.epfl.ch/index.html?content=resources/podcast/

The 50 Best Robots Ever
http://www.wired.com/wired/archive/14.01/robots.html

Acknowledgments

Special thanks to artists Catherine Heard, Andrew Harris, Chum McLeod, designer Alicia Sadler, and Peter Hansen. Warm thanks to Sheba Meland who made even rainy-day revisions a great pleasure. I am grateful to Polly Guggenheim of Personal Robots Group and James Jacobs, executor for the estate of Jane Jacobs. Big hugs to Daryn Lehoux, Zoë Lehoux, Bonnie McTaggart, Gary Bryant, and Julie Wheeler-Bryant for their active support in my writing endeavors. And thanks, especially, to all the kids who love to read, build, and create.

Photo Credits

cover (L-R): © ukinindia.fco.gov.uk, © General Motors,

© Rick Friedman/Corbis, © Frank Lennon/Toronto Star,

© Jason Szenes/epa/Corbis

page 15: © Frank Lennon/Toronto Star

page 21: © Frank Lennon/Toronto Star

page 22: © Toronto Star

page 25: © Etta Gerdes

page 35: © Kiku Hawkes

page 37: © General Motors

page 41: © General Motors

page 42: © General Motors

page 47: © Trapper Frank/Corbis

page 55: © Adam Howarth

page 57: © ukinindia.fco.gov.uk

page 64: © ukinindia.fco.gov.uk